Beyond the Broken Heart

BEYOND THE BROKEN HEART

A Journey Through Grief

LEADER GUIDE

Julie Yarbrough

This book is printed on acid-free paper.

ISBN 978-1-4267-44365

Scripture quotations are from the Common English Bible. Copyright © 2011 by the Common English Bible. All rights reserved. Used by permission. www.CommonEnglishBible.com.

Scripture quotations marked ESV are from The Holy Bible, English Standard Version® (ESV®), copyright © 2001 by Crossway, a publishing ministry of Good News Publishers. Used by permission. All rights reserved

Scripture quotations marked *THE MESSAGE* are taken from *THE MESSAGE*. Copyright © by Eugene H. Peterson 1993, 1994, 1995, 1996, 2000, 2001, 2002. Used by permission of NavPress Publishing Group.

Scripture quotations marked NASB are from the *New American Standard Bible*®, Copyright © 1960, 1962, 1963, 1968, 1971, 1972, 1973, 1975, 1977, 1995 by The Lockman Foundation. Used by permission. (www.Lockman.org)

Scripture quotations marked NIV are from the Holy Bible, New International Version®. Copyright © 1973, 1978, 1984, 2011 by Biblica, Inc.™ All rights reserved worldwide. www.zondervan.com. The "NIV" and "New International Version" are trademarks registered in the United States Patent and Tradmark Office by Biblica, Inc. ™

Scripture quotations marked NKJV are taken from the New King James Version®. Copyright © 1982 by Thomas Nelson, Inc. Used by permission. All rights reserved.

Scripture quotations marked KJV are from the authorized (King James) version. Rights in the Authorized Version in the United Kingdom are vested in the Crown. Reproduced by permission of the Crown's patentee, Cambridge University Press.

Scripture quotation marked NRSV are taken from the New Revised Standard Version of the Bible, copyright 1989, Division of Christian Education of the National Council of the Churches of Christ in the United States of America. Used by permission. All rights reserved.

Scripture quotations marked RSV are from the Revised Standard Version of the Bible, copyright 1952 [2nd edition, 1971] by the Division of Christian Education of the National Council of the Churches of Christ in the United States of America. Used by permission. All rights reserved.

12 13 14 15 16 17 18 19 20 21—10 9 8 7 6 5 4 3 2 1

MANUFACTURED IN THE UNITED STATES OF AMERICA

CONTENTS

PREFACE

In 2004 my beloved husband, Leighton Farrell, a United Methodist minister, was diagnosed with a terminal disease. He died a very short ninety days later. When he died, my heart shattered into one million small pieces.

Three months after Leighton died I was desperate for an outlet to express my grief beyond the walled-in safety of my journal. For years a neighborhood church advertised a "Grief Recovery" program on a portable billboard when sessions were forming. I called, spoke to the person in charge, and told a little of my story. Because the leader seemed rather indifferent to my need, I quickly dismissed the idea of a group with almost panicked relief.

Later that year, a pastoral care minister at my church asked "how I was doing." The dangling, painful, unspoken end of her inquiry was "without Leighton." When she saw my pain-filled tears, she gently recommended a book by a local retired Methodist clergywoman, Rev. Patsy Brundige, who, because of her own experience of loss, had become a grief specialist.

After I read the book, I asked to meet with her, hoping for a personal lifeline of help. She graciously agreed and listened thoughtfully to my outpouring of pain and sorrow. Her professional and personal interest changed the course of my grief; I often tell her that she saved my life. For you see, she understood. Her husband died when she was exactly the same age I was when Leighton died. She knew what it felt like to be 55 years old and lose a spouse.

Patsy became my grief mentor and was there for me through the darkest days and months of my grief. And over time we became friends. Her support and spiritual encouragement guided my way on the journey through grief. She was my bridge builder on the road back to life.

> *An old man going a lone highway,*
> *Came, at the evening cold and gray,*
> *To a chasm vast and deep and wide.*
> *Through which was flowing a sullen tide.*
> *The old man crossed in the twilight dim,*
> *The sullen stream had no fears for him;*
> *But he turned when safe on the other side,*
> *And built a bridge to span the tide.*

"Old man," said a fellow pilgrim near,
"You are wasting your strength with building here;
Your journey will end with the ending day;
You never again will pass this way;
You've crossed the chasm, deep and wide,
Why build this bridge at the evening tide?"

The builder lifted his old gray head;
"Good friend, in the path I have come," he said,
"There followed after me to-day
A youth whose feet must pass this way.
This chasm that has been as naught to me
To that fair-haired youth may a pitfall be;
He, too, must cross in the twilight dim;
Good friend, I am building the bridge for him!"

"The Bridge Builder," Will Allen Dromgoole (1860-1934)[1]

In grateful appreciation for her wise counsel and friendship, I made a small presentation on financial management to a group at a day-long retreat on grief that Patsy was leading. As I left, Patsy followed me to the car. She urged me to consider starting a grief group at my church. I was certain that I could never lead a group because I did not attend groups or join groups. At times my father liked to invoke this aphorism with all the wisdom of its sly double negative, "Never say what you're not going to do because that's exactly what you will end up doing." Time and again in life his little saying has proven true.

Almost two years later, I felt God gently asking me to start and lead a grief group at our church. Though it was not a loud clarion call, he gently urged me, despite my timid response, "Who, me? But God, you know that I am not a group person." Without a real plan in mind, I contacted the Pastoral Care minister at our church about starting a regular group for widows and widowers; she and her staff colleagues offered their wholehearted support.

When we began, I knew only that the group would meet bi-weekly for one hour. I did not know how many weeks or months the group would go on. I had no idea who would show up, if anyone. What I did know was that the meetings must offer spiritual, emotional, and practical support for both men and women based on the foundations of faith and scripture. I knew, too, that my leadership must be offered with utmost care and compassion for the pain of those in the group.

When the group met for the first time, those who came defied any stereo-typical notion of widow or widower. Of the twelve who were the core group for over two years, the participants were an equal number of men and women, evenly divided between young and old. The faithfulness and deep spiritual need of our group inspired me in our shared quest to both understand and grow beyond our grief.

After the group concluded, I compiled the topics we considered into a book, *Inside the Broken Heart: Grief Understanding for Widows and Widowers*. I had no idea where its publication would lead, yet God opened a door, and then another. And now you are reading words by someone certain she could never lead a group.

If you have never led a group and you are perhaps wavering about your ability or in your self-confidence, perhaps my story will encourage you to respond if this ministry is God's direction for your life. As a group leader, you offer the humanity and wisdom of a life tried and tested to those who grieve and affirm by your witness that there is life beyond the broken heart.

Julie Yarbrough
Dallas, Texas

INTRODUCTION

To survive and live forward, those who grieve must find answers. Beyond the Broken Heart is an eight-week support and ministry program for those who are grieving the loss of a loved one. Through your capable leadership, participants will find support and encouragement as they seek life in renewed hope and joy beyond the broken heart of grief.

Anyone who has a heart for those who grieve can lead a grief support group. You may be a pastor or church staff person. You may be a pastoral care volunteer or a Stephen minister. You may be a lay person who has been asked to lead a group or who has volunteered to lead one. Or you may be a professional counselor who plans to lead a group in the community or a church. To be an effective leader, it is not necessary that you have pastoral or counseling experience—only a desire to minister to those who grieve.

The program uses topical references from the Bible, video, and group discussion to illuminate the unfamiliar emotions and questions of grief over the course of eight sessions, with the option of two supplemental sessions. In either a 60- or 90-minute format, sessions can be scheduled for weekly, bi-weekly, or monthly group meetings. The program offers significant flexibility for creating a time structure that will work for your group, whether you are meeting in a church, another community location, or a home. Recommended group size is 6-12 participants.

Each group member will need a copy of *Beyond the Broken Heart: A Journey Through Grief* (hereafter called the *Participant Book)* and will read one chapter prior to each session. Each chapter in the *Participant Book* includes:

- personal reflections from the author's journey through grief
- spiritual and practical help for navigating the emotions, experiences, and questions of grief
- scriptures and biblical material appropriate to the themes and topics of each chapter
- questions for personal reflection with space for recording responses

As leader, your role will be to guide participants in their growth through grief within the sanctity of the group. Together you will explore many of the spiritual and practical issues of grief and consider specific coping strategies. Three resources will assist you in this process. The first is this *Leader Guide,* which is divided into two sections for your convenience:

1) Leader Support:
   - suggestions on forming and sustaining grief ministry
   - how-tos for promoting, planning, and facilitating a successful group experience
   - suggestions for creating a group to serve several churches or community programs
   - detailed information about starting a group
   - suggestions for effective leadership of the group
   - examples of challenges and solutions that sometimes arise within a group
   - guidelines for leading the group sessions
   - ground rules that will help you establish and maintain the integrity of the group

2) Group Sessions:
   - spiritual resources for your personal preparation before each session
   - easy-to-follow session plan outlines for eight sessions, plus two supplemental sessions on the holidays and personal finances

Each week's session plan outline will lead you step by step through the following suggested format:

Greeting
Opening Prayer
Video
Content Review
Discussion and Sharing
Summary Statement and Scripture
Closing Prayer
(See page 32 for 60- and 90-minute format options.)

The second resource you will use is the DVD, which provides eight video segments featuring the author and a licensed professional counselor. Each video segment is approximately nine to twelve minutes in length and includes:
- an introduction to the topic for the week
- two short illustrations from the author's own journey through grief to help participants relate to the session theme
- key scripture passages
- and practical points related to the session topic

The third resource you will need is the *Participant Book*. As leader, you will read the corresponding chapter prior to the group session. Using the *Participant Book* will help to prepare you for the session, particularly for the Content Review and Discussion and Sharing segments.

As leader of a grief ministry support group, you will find that those who grieve long to tell their stories so that others will understand the pivotal moments in life when their worlds forever changed. When participants open their hearts to share their stories within the sanctity of the group—certain they are heard by others who know the experience of death and grief—they will realize that they are not alone. As participants journey through "the valley of the shadow of death," Beyond the Broken Heart will help to guide the way back to fullness of life. Grief will be transformed as the group moves in community toward new life in gratitude for the steadfast love and faithfulness of God.

When you step out in faith to lead, listen, care for, and nurture those who grieve, you give the gift of yourself to others for their life beyond the broken heart.

PART I – LEADER SUPPORT

STARTING THE GROUP

Planning and Promotion

For by the grace given to me I say to everyone among you not to think of yourself more highly than you ought to think, but to think with sober judgement, each according to the measure of faith that God has assigned. For as in one body we have many members, and not all the members have the same function, so we, who are many, are one body in Christ, and individually we are members one of another. We have gifts that differ according to the grace given to us: prophecy, in proportion to faith; ministry, in ministering; the teacher, in teaching; the exhorter, in exhortation; the giver, in generosity; the leader, in diligence; the compassionate, in cheerfulness.
Romans 12:3-8 NRSV

If you are reading this *Leader Guide*, likely you are interested in starting a grief support group. You may be planning to lead it yourself, or exploring what it would take to lead a grief support group in order to recruit a capable leader. You may be a pastor or church staff person. You may be a lay pastoral care volunteer or a Stephen minister who discerns the need for a grief support group in your church. You may be a lay person who has been asked to lead a group or who has volunteered to lead one. Or you may be a professional counselor who plans to lead a group in the community or a church. But it is by no means a requirement that you have pastoral or counseling experience to be an effective grief group leader. If you have a heart for those who grieve and bring to your mission both empathy and compassion, you can lead a grief support group.

Whatever your background or motivation for starting a grief-support group, you will be equipped to lead a group using this *Leader Guide* and the DVD for each session. The following guidelines will help you start, plan, and promote a grief support group.

1. Many churches do not have a support group for those in the congregation and/or community who are grieving the death of a loved one. If you are interested in being the leader of a Beyond the Broken Heart grief group, contact the person on staff at your church who best understands this area of pastoral care.
   - If a staff person or committee needs to review and approve the Beyond the Broken Heart program, the *Leader Guide* and DVD provide a good overview of the content.
   - A kit containing one each of the program components is also available.
   - In addition, the pocket-sized *A Journey Through Grief: Life Beyond the Broken Heart* is available, which well summarizes the journey using much of the content covered in the group sessions. This inexpensive little book is a resource that might encourage those who are interested in the group but may be hesitant about participating.

2. Depending on the size of your church and/or the number of persons in the church who are grieving the loss of a loved one, it may not be possible to constitute a stand-alone group. A grief group typically is most dynamic when there are 6-12 people who participate and, over time, bond to become a real support community. If there are not enough people within your own church, consider coordinating with other churches in your community to form a joint grief group. Here are a few things to keep in mind:
   - The church most centrally located might serve as host and provide the meeting space.
   - Each church should then promote the grief support group through its newsletter, worship bulletin, website, etc.
   - To avoid any confusion, it should be made clear in all publicity that there is one location for meetings and one contact person, number, or website.
   - A joint grief group might be an interest story for media outlets. Cooperative church efforts always seem to be newsworthy.

3. Decide on a time frame for the group. There are a variety of possibilities:
   - 8 weeks – Meet once a week for 8 weeks.
   - 10 weeks – Meet weekly using the 8 sessions and the 2 supplemental sessions.
   - 16-20 weeks – Meet bi-weekly for a total of 16 or 20 weeks. Or, meet weekly but devote two sessions to each session guide. This latter option allows you to:
     - Spend more time in each session on content review and group discussion.
     - Have a more in-depth study of grief.
     - Use the same opening and closing for the two sessions, or create new ones for the additional session.

- 8-10 months – Meet consecutively once a month for 8 or 10 months.
- 12 months – Meet for 10 sessions, gathering once a month over a year with two months designated as breaks.

Note that the two supplement sessions can be used at any time during the program. Here are some ideas for incorporating these sessions:

- It is effective to use "Grief at the Holidays" during November and December.
- Each of the three topics in chapter 9 of the *Participant Book* is relatively short. A session on each topic—The Season, The Experience, The Light—would allow the group time for rich, cathartic conversation about the emotions of grief at the holiday season.
- If one session is planned before Thanksgiving and two sessions before Christmas, the group has continuous support throughout the holiday season.
- Your church might want to open the group to anyone in the community who is grieving at the holidays, whatever their experience of loss (divorce, estrangement, loss of job, death of a friend, etc.).
- The supplemental session Peace of Mind: Financial Management for Life might be offered before the New Year or as an option for "break" months or weeks, or at the end of the program after the 8 sessions have been completed. This session content is also well suited to spread out over 2-4 sessions.

Here are some things to consider when deciding on a time frame for the group:

- How many weeks or months should be scheduled?
- How does the schedule for the group coincide with events in the church liturgical year?
- Should the sessions be scheduled during the fall with a lead-in to Advent and Christmas?
- Should the group be scheduled before or after Lent or Easter?
- Would the focus on Christ's death during Lent emphasize the pain of group participants already struggling with grief and death?
- Could the sessions be scheduled to parallel the message of Holy Week and Easter? How does the schedule for the group coincide or conflict with events on the church calendar?

4. Decide on the day of the week and the time of day to meet. If your area is subject to the time shifts of Daylight Savings Time, select a time that allows older participants to attend without concern about driving after dark.
   - When would most participants likely be available to attend?
     + On a weekday?
     + On Saturday or Sunday?
     + In the late afternoon?
     + In the early evening?

- Is it practical to consider scheduling the group for a day and time when others will be at the church or venue for activities such as choir practice?

5. Schedule the time and day that the group will meet on the church calendar. The sessions are ideally structured for a 90-minute meeting, which includes time for discussion and sharing.

6. Ask your pastoral care contact or pastor to provide a list (name/phone number/email address) of those in your church or community who have experienced the death of a loved one within the past several months.

7. Contact those on the list with information about the new grief group. As the leader, respond to questions and concerns about participating in the group with your outreach of comfort and hope.

8. Encourage those who have been grieving for three months or longer to participate in the group. Most often, people whose grief is new (less than three months) are not yet ready for a group. Participating in a group immediately after the death of a loved one may be painful rather than comforting. Those who rush into a group soon after the death of a loved one may feel overwhelmed and quickly drop out.

9. When the schedule is set, confirm it on the church calendar. Identify possible participants and begin to publicize the opportunity to participate in a grief support group:
   - Prepare copy for your church newsletter or website several weeks prior to the beginning of the group. (See the sample on page 134.) This could include an image of the cover of the *Participant Book* if space allows.
   - Use social media to promote the group. If you are not familiar with this as a promotional outlet, you might want to consider consulting with someone you know who is experienced in the use of social media.
   - Place an announcement in the Sunday worship bulletin of your church with your contact information. (See the sample on page 135.)
   - Offer the group through local print media—newspapers, community calendars, community newsletters, etc. There is always someone in need of a grief support group.
   - Ask for coverage by the news media—a newspaper article or interview, a radio announcement, etc.
   - Speak to Sunday school classes or other groups in the church to promote the group to those who may want to participate or know of someone who might be interested.

- When publicizing the group, include a contact number or email address for interested participants to pre-register. You might ask the contact person on your church staff to direct calls and inquiries about registering for the group to you. This is the time to gently pre-screen participants and mention that the group is recommended for those who have been grieving for three months or longer.

10. When you know who will attend the group, make sure each person receives the *Participant Book* before the first session. Have extra books available for those who show up for the group without pre-registering. Suggest that participants read the Introduction and Chapter 1 to prepare for the first group session.

11. As you follow up after each session with those who attend, consider starting an online community where participants may interact between the sessions. Your church may have a website with secure space for a grief group community to share. Or you may want to talk with someone who can recommend the best way to establish an online place for your group to post and exchange ideas. As leader you have the opportunity to monitor and contribute regularly to the exchange of your group. Your group forum could also be used to network with other Beyond the Broken Heart leaders and/or groups.

12. If your church has a special Christmas service of remembrance, you might ask to participate in some way (reading scripture, lighting candles, etc.) to support those in the group and others in the congregation and community who are grieving at the holidays.

LEADING THE GROUP

Your Role as Leader

Now may our Lord Jesus Christ himself, and God our Father,
who loved us and gave us eternal comfort and good hope
through grace, comfort your hearts and establish them
in every good work and word.
2 Thessalonians 2:16-17 RSV

- Your *mission* as leader is to provide spiritual care and nurture for those who grieve in the safe community of a small group. This is your "work and word" as you extend eternal comfort and good hope through the power of God's grace at work through the Holy Spirit.
- Your *objective* as leader is to guide participants in the way back to a rich and full life as you encourage and direct the group. The spiritual insights and practical content of both the *Leader Guide* and *Participant Book* for Beyond the Broken Heart are based on the scriptural wisdom of the Bible, used to support each topic.
- Your *role* as leader is to direct those who come together as a group in their shared bond of grief for a loved one. For participants, there is urgency in your message of hope. Hope is the steady trajectory of the topics you will present.
- Your *function* as leader is to facilitate. There are no lessons to plan or teach; you will be presenting topical content rather than lecturing. Each chapter in the *Participant Book* provides the content for the session and each session in the *Leader Guide* provides the structure and instructions. As the leader, you will present one or more of the spiritual and emotional issues of grief and lead the group in discussion. You will also want to highlight for the group the specific coping strategies for everyday life on the journey through grief mentioned throughout the *Participant Book* and session guides.
- Your *preparation* as leader begins with yourself. Because leading a grief support group stretches you mentally, emotionally, and spiritually, a

Leader Self-care section precedes each session guide. This section provides suggestions for your spiritual preparation during the time between each group session. Each Leader Self-care section includes a selection of scriptures relevant to the topics you will present in the session, prayer meditations for your spiritual encouragement as leader, and suggestions for your reading in the *Participant Book*.

- Your *experience* as leader will influence the group. If you have grieved the death of a loved one, you are well qualified to join hands with others and communicate heart to heart. Yours is the voice of emotional and spiritual authenticity when you say to those in the group, "I hurt with you. I share your pain. I love you." However, if you have recently lost a loved one or if you feel in any way that you are "stuck" in your own grief, it is perhaps wise not to take on the challenge of leading a group. A grief group needs and depends on the emotional reliability of a compassionate leader. If you have not yet personally experienced the loss of a loved one, the *Participant Book* relates many personal stories that you as leader can use to illustrate topics or lead into discussion with the group.

- Your *spirituality* as leader will encourage participants in their faith. Your personal warmth and the gifts of grace uniquely yours will bless those who entrust their woundedness to your care and spiritual guidance through grief. Consider Isaiah 61:1-3 (NASB), which you might think of as God's standard for you as leader of the group:

> "The Spirit of the Lord GOD is upon me,
> because the LORD has anointed me
> to bring good news to the afflicted;
> he has sent me to bind up the brokenhearted,
>
> . . . .
> to comfort all who mourn
>
> . . . .
> giving them a garland instead of ashes,
> the oil of gladness instead of mourning,
> the mantle of praise instead of a spirit of fainting.
> So they will be called oaks of righteousness,
> the planting of the LORD, that He may be glorified."

KNOWING THE GROUP

Leading for Effective Group Dynamics

And the Lord's servant must not be quarrelsome but kindly to
everyone, an apt teacher, patient...
2 Timothy 2:24 NRSV

Knowing the group so that you may lead in a way that will produce the most effective group dynamic lies in your understanding of an important fact about grief. That is, no two people are ever at the same place at the same time. There is no "one size fits all" that will meet the need of each person in the group at every session. Likely there will be some in the group who are closer to acceptance; these participants usually want to understand more about life after grief. There may be others in the group who are hanging on day to day, in need of your sensitive spiritual care and encouragement.

As you assess the collective experience of the group, you will discern how best to meet participants where they are emotionally and spiritually. Under your guidance as leader, the group will become a community that cares for and supports one another. These are some of the group dynamics that you may encounter:

1. As the leader, likely your experience will be that participants usually add to the conversation as their emotions allow and dictate. Some will be eager to articulate their thoughts and feelings; others sense that sharing is uncomfortable or simply too painful. Ideally the group develops into a forum of positive interaction.

2. As leader, promote respect for the privacy and individuality of each participant's unique experience of grief. Participants should not feel pressured to contribute to the conversation. There is no imperative to speak. Assure that silence is allowed and honored. Grief does not demand its articulation.

3. Invite group participants to support the content review with comments of understanding and affirmation. Those willing to share their experiences naturally encourage other group participants.

4. Monitor and moderate the exchange of the group so that no single individual dominates the conversation. You may need to be assertive in your leadership, intervening to redirect the conversation, if necessary. For example, you might say, "Thank you for sharing that experience (or thought, or idea, or concept) with our group." Then, without hesitation, move the conversation forward by asking if anyone else has an insight to share. If not, direct the group's attention to the next question or topic.

5. Some in the group likely have a strong personal theology of death. Others may be less interested in the "why?" of death. This is a discussion that may arise. Your role as leader is to assure that each participant is respected.

   Honor the range of beliefs that may be expressed by the group without debate or dispute. Consider what you would say or do:
   - How would you moderate an exchange of ideas on the theology of death?
     + Likely there will be one or more participants who have experienced the traumatic death of a loved one (medical disappointment, tragic accident, untimely death, etc.). They may express anger and bewilderment with a question such as "Why did God let my loved one die?" Some may believe that death occurs "at one's appointed time"; others may believe that death is "God's will." Still others may believe that death happens when our "days are accomplished." This discussion requires the leader to be both thoughtful and directive by perhaps affirming that God's mystery is part of our faith; we are not meant to know or understand some things on this side of heaven.
   - How would you direct the conversation to concepts of faith rather than theology?
     + The strength of your leadership lies in the foundation of your faith. Assure group participants of God's steadfast love and faithfulness. Use the promises of the Bible highlighted in the *Participant Book, Leader Guide,* and DVD to direct the conversation away from theology toward the assurances of faith.

6. The intent of the group is to offer compassion and understanding. Whether you are a pastor, church staff member, or layperson, it is your role to assure that the collective spirit of the group is a safe, respectful, and confidential emotional environment. Only then can a spiritual community form in which participants feel free to express their pain and vulnerability.

   - As the leader, be prepared to deflect any judgment or criticism of the grief of another if it should arise.

Example:

The group has met three times. The participants are beginning to interact in openness and trust. A discernible community is forming. When a seventy-year-old woman, a lifelong church member, joins the group for the first time, she listens with obvious distraction and apparent disinterest to the leader's content review on fear and worry. During the discussion, the woman interrupts, impatiently offering her opinion on why others should not feel as they do. She insistently tells those in the group how they should "fix" their fear and worry caused by grief. The leader listens actively, observes the disruptive affect her presence is having on the group, intervenes, and quickly directs the conversation back to the topic. Although the meeting is almost over, it is clear that the safe environment of the group has been violated. When the woman attends the next meeting, the leader begins by kindly, but insistently, restating the ground rules for participating in the group (see page 36).

- The "hostage-taker" is usually one who is isolated and lonely and sees a group as the opportunity to engage a captive audience. When the "hostage taker" assumes control, the entire group is at the mercy of the seemingly inexhaustible passion of the person speaking.

  Without an awareness of the possibility for a "hostage taker" and the skill, as leader, to successfully manage and hopefully defuse the moment, the integrity of the group is at risk. Remember that an unexpected ambush momentarily disempowers you as the leader. It is a formidable challenge of leadership to restore the emotional equilibrium of a grief group once it is assaulted or breached. It is difficult for a group to recover from the intensity of a "hostage taker" situation. Some participants may drop out because of a single incident.

Example:

The group meets as scheduled. Participants faithfully attend "their" grief group for mutual care and support. The group is growing spiritually and emotionally as participants journey through grief together. In the session, the leader presents the topic; the Reflections are used to engage the group in conversation and sharing.

Until today a middle-aged man has held back. *Remember: it is not imperative that everyone in the group speak or join into the conversation.* Unexpectedly, a question incites him. He takes the floor and holds forth in anger and at great length—hardly pausing for breath—about the medical conditions and circumstances of his wife's death. Others in the group have experienced a similar trauma; they do not want to revisit this particular pain of their grief as part of the group experience. The leader at last interrupts and brings the meeting to an unsatisfactory close.

As the leader, work to prevent setbacks for the group by assessing, if possible, the likelihood of a participant to use the group as a personal forum to vent. You do this by listening intently to the tone and attitude of the group discussion and how the possible "hostage taker" contributes. To end a tirade, be ready to act in the split second the offender must pause for breath. Intervene decisively with a kind but strong comment such as, "Yes, many of us have experienced the traumatic (sudden, tragic, etc.) death of our loved ones." Then (without pausing for breath) direct the focus to a scripture on peace or love or faith with a statement such as, "And the Bible teaches us to 'Bear with one another and, if anyone has a complaint against another, forgive each other; just as the Lord has forgiven you, so you also must forgive'" (Colossians 3:13 NRSV).

7. The group is not designed as a substitute for professional therapy or intervention. If someone in the group seems in obvious need of medical or psychiatric help, ask a pastoral care professional for assistance with resources for the one in distress. Some indications of the need for immediate help may include extreme agitation, unusual emotional volatility, uncontrolled outbursts, uninterrupted weeping, dizziness, fainting, slurred speech, obvious drug or alcohol abuse, or other apparent signs of physical and/or mental compromise. If necessary, call 911 for help. In all likelihood, the group is not the place or venue to care for this person.

8. Be aware of these behaviors that are normal in grief:
   • Crying or weeping in short yet often intense bursts, with or without a slight display of temper. Usually these tears subside in a few seconds or minutes when they are spent.
   • Moderate anger that usually expresses itself as a sense of injustice, and questions such as "Why did she have to die?" or "Why did he die and not me?"
   • Mood swings between sorrow and hope, pain and joy, defensiveness and trust.
   • Fear expressed as anxiety, helplessness, or insecurity. Mild, temporary panic attacks are not uncommon in grief.
   • Sadness and loneliness, which are the nature of grief.
   • Physical symptoms such as fatigue, nausea, lowered immunity, weight loss or weight gain, aches and pains, and insomnia.

HEARING THE GROUP

Active Listening Strategies

Let anyone with ears listen!
Matthew 11:15 NRSV

God listens. God hears. In order for you as leader to hear what the group is saying collectively and individually, it is important to listen with both your mind and heart.

1. Listen for understanding.
   - Hear what each individual says; each story is very personal.
   - No two people have the same experience of death and loss.

2. Listen with sensitivity.
   - Your empathy as leader will enable you to assess and adapt quickly to the emotional needs of participants.
   - Direct the group with a positive spirit of compassion and sympathy that reflects your understanding of the pain of participants.

3. Listen without judgment.
   - Allow participants to express guilt and self-recrimination about the circumstances of death.
   - Maintain your focus on compassion and understanding.

4. Listen in silence.
   - Think along with others as they speak.
   - Honor time for introspection and reflection.
   - Allow pauses and moments of silence.
   - Speak from the heart.

5. Listen with direction.
   - Ideally you will have a plan for how you intend to present the topics. As participants respond and share, realize that your plan may require redirection.

- Be prepared to accommodate the momentum and dynamic of the group as you sense a shift in focus.

6. Listen with discernment.
   - Ask open-ended questions, that is, ones that cannot be answered simply with yes, no, or maybe.
   - A well-considered question often leads a participant to understand what his or her inner voice is communicating. A productive answer is the self-help of grief.

7. Listen with compassion.
   - The need for someone to listen and understand is at the heart of grief.
   - Those who grieve need to be heard.
   - When you listen with compassion to the pain of others, you give the gift of yourself.

8. Listen for the voice of God.
   - Lead through the presence of the Holy Spirit in your mission and ministry of grief.
   - Remember that as the leader, God is at work in and through you.

LEADER GUIDELINES

What to Do Before, During, and After a Group Session

Now you are the body of Christ and individually members of it. And God has appointed in the church first apostles, second prophets, third teachers; then deeds of power, then gifts of healing, forms of assistance, forms of leadership, various kinds of tongues. Are all apostles? Are all prophets? Are all teachers? Do all work miracles? Do all possess gifts of healing? Do all speak in tongues? Do all interpret? But strive for the greater gifts. And I will show you a still more excellent way.
1 Corinthians 12:27-31 NRSV

As leader, you may be a professional teacher, academician, experienced Sunday school teacher, or church leader. If so, likely you are comfortable with leading a group and know what it takes to make the most of shared time together. Or you may have less experience in leading a group, yet you are passionate about ministering to those who grieve. Whatever your background or leadership experience may be, those who grieve need your emotional and spiritual guidance on the journey through grief.

Your success as leader of a grief support group depends on your preparation. Those who attend a grief support group are seeking both practical information and the spiritual substance to help them understand and ultimately resolve their grief. By preparing thoughtfully using both the *Leader Guide* and *Participant Book*, you will be well able to meet the group at its spiritual and emotional place of need, one that is unique to those who grieve. You honor the presence of those who attend by preparing for each meeting intentionally and prayerfully.

Here are some practical guidelines for before, during, and after a group session.

Before the Session

1. Use the Leader Self-care section for your personal spiritual preparation during the time between each group session. A scripture, reading, and prayer are offered for each day.

2. Review the session guide.
   - Each session is designed, ideally, to be 90 minutes. This is usually a manageable amount of time for participants, whose attention span may be limited by the physical, mental, and emotional demands of grief. If time constraints or other considerations make a 90-minute session impractical for your group, you may reduce the session to 60 minutes by eliminating the group activity and reducing the time allowed for content review and group discussion (follow the time suggestions provided in the session guide).
   - A time range is suggested for each segment of the session. These are suggestions only—general parameters you may want to adapt and modify to meet the needs of the group and your own leadership style.

60-Minute Session

Greeting (3–4 minutes)
Opening Prayer (1–2 minutes)
Video (9–12 minutes)
Content Review (15–18 minutes)
Discussion and Sharing (15 minutes)
Summary Statement and Scripture (2 minutes)
Closing Prayer (1–3 minutes)

90-Minute Session

Greeting (3–4 minutes)
Opening Prayer (1–2 minutes)
Video (9–12 minutes)
Content Review (30 minutes)
Discussion and Sharing (30–35 minutes)
Summary Statement and Scripture (2 minutes)
Closing Prayer (1–3 minutes)

3. Read the chapter in the *Participant Book* that corresponds to each session. Choose the topics you will review and discuss at each session and familiarize yourself with the content. It is suggested that you select 3–4 topics to cover in one group session. (If you are extending the program, devoting two group sessions to each session guide [8 sessions become 16 sessions; 10 sessions become 20 sessions], you will be able to cover most if not all of the topics in the *Participant Book*.)
   - The time for content review will vary slightly for each session, depending on the number of topics you choose to cover.
   - The objective is to balance the content review time with the discussion and sharing time.

4. If possible, preview the video for the session.

5. Ensure that the meeting place is a comfortable, nurturing environment.
- Furnish water; this is helpful to participants both physically and emotionally for moments when emotions surge.
- Put out two or more boxes of tissues within easy reach of group members to dry the inevitable tears of grief.
- Make sure there is equipment in the meeting room to play the DVD.
- Know how to use the DVD player and adjust the volume before the meeting begins.
- If needed, turn on the subtitle feature of the DVD.
- Review the setup of the room.
  - Arrange tables and/or chairs so that participants have sufficient personal space.
  - Tables allow participants to open and refer to the *Participant Book* easily.
  - Assure that the physical arrangement is conducive to conversation and interaction.

6. Review the ground rules (see page 36). Before the first group session, make copies to distribute to the group. Read or review the ground rules with the group at the start of the first session and periodically thereafter as needed.

During the Session

1. Start on time.

2. Following the format suggested in the session guide, begin with a word of greeting and inclusion to the full group (3–5 minutes).
- Be thoughtful in your choice of words, remembering that for many, being "welcomed" to a grief group creates resistance. Most participants are struggling with the reality of death; they want their lives back.
- As you greet participants, you will sense their level of pain and heartache. Your words of greeting and inclusion at the beginning of each session should be warm and genuine—speak from your heart. Acknowledge the emotional vulnerability that many in the group may be feeling. You might say, "Thank you for your willingness to be part of our grief support group. I hope that your experience within the safe community of friends will offer you comfort and hope as we journey together through grief."

3. Open the session with prayer (1–2 minutes). You will find that prayer centers the group and draws participants into the moment. Use the prayers suggested for each session or adapt the words and spiritual direction to your personal prayer vocabulary. Pray for the presence of the Holy Spirit.

4. Play the video (9–12 minutes). At the end of each video a scripture passage transitions to the content review segment.

5. Following the suggestions in the session guide, lead a content review of the topics you have chosen to cover (90-minute session: 30 minutes; 60-minute session: 15–18 minutes). After the first session you likely will have a feel for the range of grief experiences represented in the group. The *Participant Book* and session guides are structured so that you may "mix and match" the topics in each chapter to customize the content in a way that best accommodates the group.
   - Be personable and engaging in your review of the content.
   - Be sensitive to the needs of the group.
   - Throughout the content review, emphasize the scriptures used to illustrate and reinforce the topics.

6. Use the Personal Reflection questions or a suggested exercise to start and direct group discussion (90-minute session: 30-35 minutes; 60-minute session: 15 minutes).

7. After you have reviewed the topics, led the discussion, and allowed time for the group to share, the meeting is effectively over. End the group with a summary statement and scripture related to the topic (2 minutes), followed by a final prayer (1–3 minutes). If the session ends without a takeaway thought and a concluding prayer, there may be no sense of closure. As the leader, be intentional about ending the meeting so that participants leave with a sense of benefit and benediction.

8. End on time. If you sense that the session may exceed the scheduled time, invite those who want to continue their conversation after the closing prayer to stay.

After the Session

1. It is not unusual to see individuals gathered together after a meeting in groups of twos or threes. Allow participants to linger after the meeting. If possible, plan to stay and be available to them for an additional 15–20 minutes. If the church is otherwise empty or if you need to leave and participants want to continue their sharing, encourage them to go to a nearby coffee shop or informal venue to talk further. In a more intimate setting, individuals share personal details that they might not articulate to the group; they support and encourage

each other privately. It is an ideal outcome of the group experience when bonds of friendship form from the common experience of death and grief. You are an effective leader when the sanctity of the group inspires personal relationships beyond the group.

2. As leader you will observe how those in your group express their emotions. If anyone seems overwrought or unusually distressed when leaving the meeting, you might follow up with a telephone call of care and concern the next day. Likely something that was said triggered a powerful emotional response, or it might have been a personal remembrance day for the participant. Don't personalize someone else's emotions—probably you did not cause the reaction. Be sensitive and kind in your outreach. Try to discern without asking directly whether the one in distress might need or want the help of a pastor or professional. If participating in the group is too overwhelming, gently suggest that it might not be the right time in their grief journey for a group. Give them implied permission to resign. No one will think less of them for making this self-care decision.

3. As your group forms, you will get a sense of who your core participants are— those who attend regularly and are committed to the grief community. Likely there will be others who come perhaps once or twice to "try on" the group to see if it fits their needs. It is important to value the interest of each participant whenever and for however long he or she chooses to be part of the group. You might want to call or send an e-mail to anyone absent from the meeting, or follow up with new participants with a word of warm inclusion.

4. After each session, you might want to prepare a brief but concise written summary of the content. This could be used with regular participants who have missed sessions. For those who might show up for the group randomly or at later sessions (after session 4), it is not necessary for you to stop and devote session time to "catching up" one or more individuals. If you have formulated a brief summary of previous session content, you could share this with new participants in a 1–2 minute "elevator speech."

> *But each of us was given grace according to the measure of*
> *Christ's gift. . . . The gifts he gave were that some would be*
> *apostles, some prophets, some evangelists, some pastors and*
> *teachers, to equip the saints for the work of ministry, for build-*
> *ing up the body of Christ, until all of us come to the unity of*
> *the faith and of the knowledge of the Son of God, to maturity,*
> *to the measure of the full stature of Christ.*
> Ephesians 4:7, 11-13 NRSV

GROUND RULES

- Our group is not a venue for "fixing" the problems of another person, even though our suggestions may be well-intentioned.

- We encourage the open exchange of feelings and emotions in our group.

- Our group honors those who prefer to listen rather than share.

- Our group agrees to protect the confidentiality of others.

- Our conversations begin and end within our group—what we say here does not leave the group.

- We agree that whatever we share will not become the subject of church talk or gossip.

- We respect the privacy of our group members. This a non-negotiable point of group behavior and integrity.

Reproduced by permission from Julie Yarbrough, *Beyond the Broken Heart: A Journey Through Grief, Leader Guide* (Nashville: Abingdon Press, 2012).

PART II – GROUP SESSIONS

SESSION 1 – NAMING GRIEF

Leader Self-care

(A guide for your spiritual preparation prior to Session 1)

The human mind plans the way, but the LORD directs the steps.
Proverbs 16:9 NRSV

Day 1:
Reflect: "The eternal God is your refuge, and underneath are the everlasting arms" (Deuteronomy 33:27 NIV).

Read: What is Grief?—*Participant Book,* pages 14–17

Pray: Pray for God's blessing on your leadership.

Day 2:
Reflect: "Let everyone be quick to listen, slow to speak, slow to anger; for your anger does not produce God's righteousness" (James 1:19-20 NRSV).

Read: Anger—*Participant Book,* pages 17–21

Pray: Pray for your calmness of spirit as you encounter anger within your group.

Day 3:
Reflect: "Out of my distress I called on the Lord; the Lord answered me and set me free. With the Lord on my side I do not fear. What can man do to me?" (Psalm 118:5-6 RSV).

Read: Fear—*Participant Book,* pages 21–24

Pray: Pray that God will make you a fearless leader.

Day 4:
Reflect: "Do not worry about your life" (Matthew 6:25 NRSV).

Read: Worry—*Participant Book,* pages 25–27

Pray: Pray that God will quiet your worry about your leadership.

Day 5:
Reflect: "For the Lord has comforted his people, and will have compassion on his suffering ones" (Isaiah 49:13 NRSV).

Read: Suffering—*Participant Book,* pages 27–32

Pray: Pray that God will attune your heart to the suffering of those in your group.

Day 6:
Reflect: "Rejoice always, pray without ceasing, give thanks in all circumstances; for this is the will of God in Christ Jesus for you" (1 Thessalonians 5:15-18 NRSV).

Read: Prayer—*Participant Book,* pages 33–36

Pray: Pray that God will encourage you in your leadership.

Day 7:
Reflect: "Rejoice in hope, be patient in suffering, persevere in prayer" (Romans 12:12 NRSV).

Read: Introduction—*Leader Guide,* pages 11–13

Pray: Pray you will be established in God's hope as you lead those who grieve.

Session Outline

Greeting (3-4 minutes)
- Begin with a warm word of greeting and inclusion to the entire group. Remember that, for many, being "welcomed" to a grief group creates resistance. Most participants are struggling with the reality of death; they want their life back (see Leader Support page 33).

- Be thoughtful in your choice of words. It is always easier to advance than retreat when establishing a group. You will discover how best to engage with the group as you begin to assess and understand the emotions of the group, both individually and collectively.

- Take a few minutes to review and establish the ground rules for the group (see page 36). You may want to distribute copies. Participants will visibly relax when they know that there is safety in the group and structure for the group. Keep additional copies and distribute to those who join the group from time to time.

Opening Prayer (1-2 minutes)
God, we give you thanks for those who gather together here today to share in community the pain of grief. We pray that you will open every grief-laden heart to the inspiration and guidance of your holy word. In the sanctity of our group, may we understand sorrow as we prepare to live in joy again. Amen.

Video (9-12 minutes)
Play the video for Session 1.

Content Review
(90-minute session: 30 minutes; 60-minute session: 15-18 minutes)

Choose from the following six topics according to the time available and the needs of your group.

What Is Grief? (5-7 minutes)
- Read aloud the following scripture:

  I tell you the truth, you will weep and mourn while the world rejoices. You will grieve, but your grief will turn to joy. (John 16:20 NIV)

- Reiterate the definition of grief: *Grief is the outpouring of emotion and pain that expresses how you feel because of what has happened in your life.*

- Select 3-5 of the "Grief is . . ." points on page 14 in the *Participant Book*. Read each point aloud and ask the group a question such as, "Does this describe your experience of grief?" (Note: Although this is a "closed-ended" question—easily answered with "yes" or "no"—this is the first time you are asking group members to respond. Participants may be eager or reluctant to share; some may hold back until they get a feel for others in the group. If there is no response other than nods and murmurs, you might ask if someone would like to share a specific instance that illustrates, for example, a time when he or she started to speak to someone who is no longer there. If there is still no response, move quickly to the next part of the presentation.)

- Affirm these points from the video:
  - Grief is not a crisis of faith.
  - Grief is a crisis of the heart.
  - We grieve because we love.

- Summarize the concept of grief as a show of faith (*Participant Book* page 16) and encourage a brief time of sharing.

Anger (5-7 minutes)
- Read aloud the following scripture:

  Peace I leave with you; my peace I give to you. I do not give to you as the world gives. Do not let your hearts be troubled, and do not let them be afraid. (John 14:27 NRSV)

- Assure the group that anger is a common emotional reflex to separation from the one loved and lost in death.

- Help the group identify the reasons for anger (*Participant Book* page 18). Make these points about anger:
  - Anger may surprise you with its force and power.
  - You are not prepared for anger's full frontal assault on your heart.
  - Anger thrives and consumes vital energy if you provide a place in your heart for it to take root and grow.
  - Anger is a manageable, short-term reaction to the death of your loved one.

  ❖ Anger is a normal response to the injustice of death.
  ❖ Anger is a by-product of grief.

- Offer these solutions for anger:
  ❖ Instead of nurturing anger, name it and confront it.
  ❖ When you identify your unresolved issues of guilt and regret, you are able to release them.
  ❖ It is easier to release anger than to hold on to it.
  ❖ You feel immediate relief when you forsake anger.

- As time allows, use one or more of the Personal Reflections on pages 20–21 of the *Participant Book* to lead a short discussion about anger. (Note: Guilt and regrets are the topic for Discussion and Sharing later in the session.)
  ❖ What are the personal issues of grief that make you angry?
  ❖ What is the reason for your anger?
  ❖ What purpose does your anger serve?
  ❖ How is your anger affecting you and others?
  ❖ What are you doing to identify and resolve your anger?

Fear (5-7 minutes)
- Read aloud the following scripture:

  Fear not, for I am with you, be not dismayed, for I am your God; I will strengthen you, I will help you, I will uphold you with my victorious right hand. (Isaiah 41:10 RSV)

- Read aloud the definition of fear: Fear is "a feeling of agitation and anxiety; a feeling of disquiet or apprehension."[2] (Note: As leader, you may find the definitions and other factual information throughout the *Participant Book* helpful for focusing participants on the known, as opposed to the vast unknowns of grief. Try it as a leadership device; see if this has a centering effect on the group.)

- Talk with the group about the fears they are encountering in grief (see below). As you name these common fears, participants likely will want to interject affirmations, comments, and personal experiences. General fears:
  ❖ fear of illness and death
  ❖ fear of change
  ❖ fear of the unknown
  ❖ fear of the future

Personal fears:
  + fear of not having enough money
  + fear of driving
  + fear of living without your loved one
  + fear of going to public places
  + fear of loneliness
  + fear that you will get hurt
  + fear that you will die alone or lose someone else close to you

- Introduce the practice of journaling as a possibility for managing the fear of grief (*Participant Book* page 22). Bring one or more books to show what a journal looks like (a spiral notebook, a book of blank pages, a notepad, or anything with space for writing). There will be some in the group who journal regularly; others may be unfamiliar with journaling or have some resistance to writing. Emphasize that when you write about fear,
  + You face it.
  + You put it in perspective.
  + You consign it to a safe, private place.
  + You assess whether it is real.
  + You recognize it as the temporary by-product of life in constant change.

- Encourage participants to spend time in the days ahead considering the Personal Reflections on page 24 in the *Participant Book*.

- Close with these affirmations about fear:
  When you do what you fear,
  + You turn it into courage.
  + You disable its power.
  + You defeat it.
  + You become stronger.

Worry (5-7 minutes)
- Read aloud the following scripture:

  Therefore do no worry about tomorrow, for tomorrow will worry about itself. Each day has enough trouble of its own. (Matthew 6:34 NIV)

- Break down worry by making a clear distinction of the various degrees of worry (*Participant Book* pages 25–26). Affirm that
  + the emotional pain of grief intensifies worry.
  + fear inspires worry.

    ✤ anxiety is worry intensified.

    ✤ agonizing is the most extreme form of worry.

- Use the questions on pages 26–27 in the *Participant Book* to illustrate the gradations of worry.

- Talk with participants about their ongoing conversation of the mind. Likely they will agree that they are aware of a circular inner monologue that goes on most of the time. (Note: Participants will be reassured to hear others affirm that this is a distraction of grief that nurtures their worry. The group begins to form into a community when participants are assured by others that they are experiencing similar struggles and challenges in grief.)

- As time allows, select one or more questions from the Personal Reflections (*Participant Book* pages 26–27) to lead a short conversation about worry.

- Close with the affirmation that worry is a side effect of grief, not a permanent condition.
  - ✤ Suggest that worry can be defeated and conquered through persistent prayer, quiet introspection, and personal meditation.
  - ✤ Assure the group: God is larger than your worry.

Suffering (5-7 minutes)

- Read aloud the following scripture:

  But those who suffer he delivers in their suffering; he speaks to them in their affliction. (Job 26:15 NIV)

- Restate one of the overarching themes of the session highlighted in the video: *We grieve because we love.* (Note: By "connecting the dots" for participants with linear logic and definitions, often this answers the "why" for the group. As leader, use the practical information provided in the *Participant Book* to balance the emotional complexity of grief.) Communicate the following points:
  - ✤ If we did not love, we would not suffer.
  - ✤ The more sensitive we are, the more we suffer.
  - ✤ When we grieve, we suffer the pain of loss.
  - ✤ Physical suffering is often a manifestation of grief; grief and suffering are inextricably linked.
  - ✤ Suffering is part of life. It is part of what it means to be human.

- Focus the group on Job, whose life experience supports the topic of suffering (*Participant Book* pages 27–32). Lead a short, guided conversation on the suffering of Job. Start with the question "Why did God allow Job to suffer?" If time allows, ask this additional question, "What is the spiritual lesson we who are grieving learn from Job's suffering?"

- Consider with the group the various meanings of *suffering* (*Participant Book* page 29).

- The suffering of grief includes enduring the attitudes and superficial platitudes offered as comfort, which hurt rather than help. Lead through this theme by selecting some of the attitudes and platitudes often heard by those who grieve (*Participant Book* pages 29–30).

- As time allows, use one or more of these questions modified from the Personal Reflections on page 32 of the *Participant Book* (or others of your choosing) to lead a short discussion on suffering in grief. (Note: Participants likely will offer some impassioned answers and comments. Those who have suffered the well-intentioned words of others need the opportunity to express the hurt of their suffering.)
  + What words have you suffered that hurt instead of helped?
  + Have you forgiven the well-intentioned comforter who spoke them?
  + What have you learned from your suffering that will enable you to be a more sensitive comforter?

- Encourage the group with the assurance of 1 Peter 5:10: "And after you have suffered for a little while, the God of all grace, who has called you to his eternal glory in Christ, will himself restore, support, strengthen, and establish you" (NRSV). Point out that although the verse affirms that you will suffer "for a little while," it is not God's intention that you suffer forever. Assure the group that "a little while" is not forever and encourage them to be intentional about patience in grief "for a little while." Say: "God is with you in and through your suffering. You will not always suffer."

Prayer (5-7 minutes)
- Read aloud the following scripture:

  I love the Lord, because he has heard my voice and my supplications. Because he inclined his ear to me, therefore I will call on him as long as I live. The snares of death encompassed me; . . . I suffered distress and anguish. Then I called on the name of the LORD: "O LORD, I pray, save my life!" (Psalm 116:1-4 NRSV)

- Assure the group that prayer is one of the most confusing aspects of grief. Acknowledge the following:

- ✦ When your emotions are in turmoil, it is difficult to focus the mind and spirit to pray.
- ✦ You may want to pray yet find no peaceful place within when your heart is consumed by anxiety and fear.
- ✦ Often there are no other words except "Lord, help me" (Matthew 15:25 NRSV).

- Talk with the group about how their expectations of prayer may have changed because of the experience of the death of a loved one. Use the Personal Reflections on pages 33–34 of the *Participant Book* to illustrate. Acknowledge that:
  - ✦ Participants may have watched their loved one die and may feel spiritually debilitated by their helplessness to change the outcome.
  - ✦ They may feel unable to pray. It may seem impossible to ask for or receive answers to prayer.

- Make these points with the group:
  - ✦ The answer to prayer may be wait or no.
  - ✦ The answer is always yes when you pray for comfort and strength.
  - ✦ All prayers are answered.
  - ✦ If you feel disconnected from God, allow the prayers of others to carry you for a while.
  - ✦ Prayer alleviates spiritual weariness.
  - ✦ Prayer reminds you that you are dependent on God and not on yourself.
  - ✦ Through prayer you grow spiritually.

- Reflect with the group on the faithfulness of the psalmists in prayer. They offered their impassioned cries to God for others and about others from the same place of personal loneliness and isolation that we experience in grief. Affirm the following:
  - ✦ God listens: "But God has surely listened and heard my voice in prayer" (Psalm 66:19 NIV).
  - ✦ God is always there.
  - ✦ God hears you when you pray and reaches into your heart with abiding comfort and strength.

Discussion and Sharing
(90-minute session: 30-35 minutes; 60-minute session: 15 minutes)

Use this time to engage the group in discussion about regret and guilt (*Participant Book* pages 19–20). This is an important topic for many who grieve, especially in the resolution of other emotions of grief (e.g., anger, fear, worry). Use the Personal Reflections on page 20 in the *Participant Book* to begin a discussion of the "might have been" and the "could, would, should" of guilt in grief. Encourage group members to name their guilt and regrets, either privately or by sharing with the group. Acknowledge that identifying the unresolved issues of guilt and regret may be painful. Affirm that it is a first step in restoring order and peace in the heart.

Summary Statement and Scripture (2 minutes)
- When you grieve, you must feel what you feel for a while.
- When you name the emotions and feelings of grief, you release them in faithful prayer to God.
- God is with you in and through the suffering of grief.
- You will not always suffer.
- You are not alone in your grief.

Now is your time of grief, but I will see you again and you will rejoice, and no one will take away your joy. (John 16:22 NIV)

Closing Prayer (1-3 minutes)
Use the following prayer, offer one of your own, or invite a group member to pray. Or, if your group prefers, allow the group to share prayer concerns and pray for one another.

God, as we leave this gathering of our grief community, we offer this meditation in thanksgiving for your abiding presence to us as we grieve: "For those who walked with us, this is a prayer. For those who have gone ahead, this is a blessing. For those who have touched and tended us, who lingered with us while they lived, this is a thanksgiving. For those who journey still with us in the shadows of awareness, in the crevices of memory, in the landscape of our dreams, this is a benediction."[3]

SESSION 2: UNDERSTANDING GRIEF

Leader Self-care

(A guide for your spiritual preparation prior to Session 2)

I am the good shepherd. The good shepherd lays down his life for the sheep.
John 10:11 NRSV

Day 1:
Reflect: "The LORD is my shepherd, I shall not want" (Psalm 23:1 RSV).

Read: Introduction to Understanding Grief—*Participant Book,* pages 39–40

Pray: Pray that God will enlighten your role as shepherd.

Day 2:
Reflect: "He makes me lie down in green pastures" (Psalm 23:2 RSV).

Read: The Stages of Grief—*Participant Book,* pages 40–44

Pray: Pray for your understanding of the stages of grief.

Day 3:
Reflect: "He leads me beside still waters" (Psalm 23:2 RSV).

Read: The Journey of Grief—*Participant Book,* page 45 (through author's reflection)

Pray: Pray that God will bless your direction as shepherd with peace.

Day 4:
Reflect: "He leads me in paths of righteousness for his name's sake" (Psalm 23:3b RSV).

Read: The Journey of Grief—*Participant Book,* pages 45–47 ("When we grieve . . ." through author's reflection on page 47)

Pray: Pray that God will show you the path of righteousness.

Day 5:
Reflect: "Surely goodness and mercy shall follow me all the days of my life" (Psalm 23:6 RSV).

Read: The Journey of Grief—*Participant Book,* pages 47–50 (up to The Journey of Grief diagram)

Pray: Pray for God's mercy and goodness as you shepherd those who grieve.

Day 6:
Reflect: "I shall dwell in the house of the LORD for ever" (Psalm 23:6 RSV).

Read: The Journey of Grief—*Participant Book,* pages 50–53 (The Journey of Grief diagram to the end)

Pray: Pray that the good shepherd will strengthen you in your faith.

Day 7:
Reflect: "He restores my soul" (Psalm 23:3a RSV).

Read: Review The Journey of Grief—*Participant Book,* pages 45–53

Pray: Pray that God will prepare you to be a spiritual shepherd for the group.

Session Outline

Greeting (3-4 minutes)
- Begin with a warm word of greeting and inclusion to the entire group. There may be some participants new to the group. Remember that, for many, being "welcomed" to a grief group creates resistance. Most participants are struggling with the reality of death; they want their life back (see Leader Support page 33).

- You may want to take a minute or two to review a few of the most important ground rules with the group and hand a copy to anyone who was not at Session 1 (see page 36). You will observe participants visibly relax when they know that there is safety in the group and structure for the group.

Opening Prayer (1-2 minutes)
Use the following prayer or adapt the words and spiritual direction to your personal prayer vocabulary.

God, we gather together because we want to understand the pain and heartache of grief. We are ready to walk hand in hand with you on the journey through grief because we trust your love and care for us. We pray for the direction and peace of the Holy Spirit as you guide the way in which we should go. Amen.

Video (9-12 minutes)
Play the video for Session 2.

Content Review
(90-minute session: 30 minutes; 60-minute session: 15–18 minutes)

Choose from the following topics according to the time available and the needs of your group.

The Stages of Grief (3-5 minutes)
- Many in the group may be familiar with the stages of grief: denial and isolation, anger, bargaining, depression, and acceptance.

- Make the point that the stages are often used to describe the clinical structure of dying, death, and grief.

- Recommend the group read the narrative describing the grief of David on pages 41–44 of the *Participant Book* as a good illustration of the stages of grief (see also Samuel 12:15-23).

The Journey of Grief (15-25 minutes)
- Read aloud the following scripture:

  Even though I walk through the valley of the shadow of death, I fear no evil, for thou art with me. (Psalm 23:4 RSV)

- Using the imagery of the scripture, affirm and expand on these points from the video:
  ✤ *Even though I walk:* Grief is a very personal journey of the heart and soul.
  ✤ *I fear no evil:* The solitary journey of grief is blessed by those who travel with you and alongside you.
  ✤ *Thou art with me:* God is our most faithful companion on the journey through grief.

- Review the various aspects of the journey of grief with the group:
  ✤ When does the journey begin?
  ✤ What is the destination of the journey?
  ✤ What are the challenges along the way?
    - Unexpected setbacks are detours.
    - Unplanned side trips through illness or disability can interrupt the journey.
    - Emotional ups and downs are the uneven pavement of a bumpy road.
    - Interactions with those who do not understand grief are the rough shoulders of a narrow, less-traveled highway.

- As time allows, use one or more of these questions modified from the Personal Reflections on page 51 of the *Participant Book* (or others of your choosing) to lead a short discussion about the starting point of the individual journey of grief:
  ✤ Did you jump off a cliff into the valley of the shadow of death because of the sudden illness or death of your loved one?
  ✤ Were you overwhelmed by a landslide of illness that went nowhere but down?
  ✤ Were you a caretaker or caregiver for several years before the death of your loved one?
  ✤ Is your grief map one that reflects persistent erosion?

- Continue with this question: How do we traverse the valley of the shadow of death?
  - ❖ Affirm that the psalmist is clear; he shares the wisdom of his experience when he answers the "how."
  - ❖ "Even though I walk . . ." Point out that we are not asked to jog, run, or race; we walk.
  - ❖ The journey through grief is slow, laborious foot work.
  - ❖ Sometimes we attempt great bounding strides.
  - ❖ The slow, steady pace of a rhythmic walk ultimately sees us through to the other side.
  - ❖ Along the way, we acquire the courage and strength for life after loss.

- Read aloud the following scripture:

  For we walk by faith, not by sight. (2 Corinthians 5:7 RSV)

- Reaffirm and expand on these points from the video:
  - ❖ W*e walk by faith.*
    - – We put one foot in front of the other.
    - – Often we walk only one half-step at a time.
  - ❖ W*e get up in faith.*
    - – We lose our balance.
    - – We miss a step.
    - – Our footing slips.
    - – We fall down.
  - ❖ *We walk in faith.*
    - – We recover our toehold.
    - – We again inch forward.
    - – We gain ground after each setback.

- As time allows, use one or more of these questions modified from the Personal Reflections on page 53 of the *Participant Book* (or others of your choosing) to lead a short discussion about the individual journey of grief:
  - ❖ Where have you been?
  - ❖ Where are you now?
  - ❖ What are your obstacles along the way?
  - ❖ If you have been on the journey for a while, are you moving forward?

Discussion and Sharing
(90-minute session: 30–35 minutes; 60-minute session: 15 minutes)

- Use this time to discuss in detail the "Journey of Grief" illustration on page 50 of the *Participant Book*. Highlight these aspects of the picture:

  * The weather
    – sunny
    – cloudy
    – stormy
    – overcast
  * The landscape
    – trees
    – grass
    – bare patches
    – undergrowth
    – briars
  * The terrain
    – rough
    – dry
    – muddy
    – wet
    – flooded
  * The depth
    – Is it steep?
    – Are there plateaus?
    – Is there a bottom?
    – How far is it to the other side?

- In advance, make copies of the "Journey of Grief" on page 56. (This version does not have the descriptive words that appear with the diagram on page 50 in the *Participant Book*.) Distribute copies to the group.

- Provide a colored pencil or pen to each participant.

- Ask participants to spend thoughtful time considering the words that describe their personal places and experiences on the journey through the valley of the shadow of death.

- Then have them complete the illustration to create pictures of their own journeys of grief, adding words and details of their choosing.

- Ask participants to share their thoughts and descriptive words.

Summary Statement and Scripture (2 minutes)
- God directs your life on the journey through grief.
- God leads you through the valley of the shadow of death.
- God guides you along the way and slowly directs you toward spiritual safety and home.

I walk before the LORD in the land of the living. (Psalm 116:9 NRSV)

Closing Prayer (1–3 Minutes)

Use the following prayer, offer one of your own, or invite a group member to pray. Or, if your group prefers, allow the group to share prayer concerns and pray for one another.

God, we understand that your divine destination for us at the end of our journey is peace. We are grateful for our time together to share the journey of grief. We learn from those who walk with us in faith through the valley of the shadow of death. We pray that as we depart today, you will direct us in our grief toward your spiritual safety and home. Amen.

The Journey of Grief

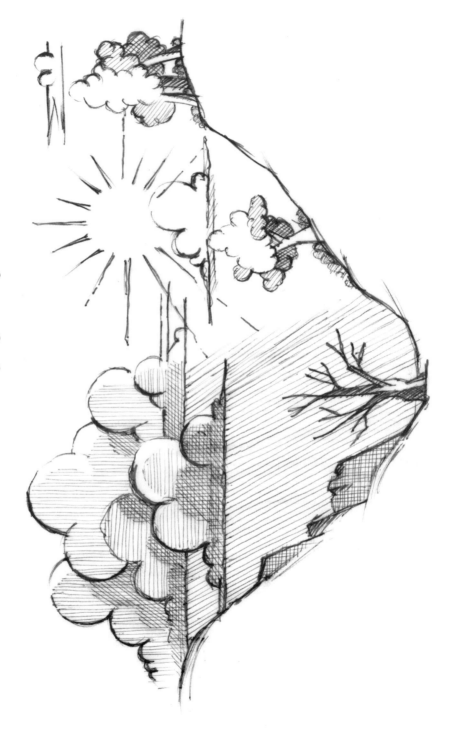

Reproduced by permission from Julie Yarbrough, *Beyond the Broken Heart: A Journey Through Grief, Leader Guide* (Nashville: Abingdon Press, 2012).

Session 3: Yielding to Grief

Leader Self-care

(A guide for your spiritual preparation prior to Session 3)

The Lord God has given me the tongue of a teacher, that I may know how to sustain the weary with a word.
Isaiah 50:4 NRSV

Day 1:
Reflect: "For I the Lord do not change" (Malachi 3:6 NRSV).

Read: Introduction to Yielding to Grief—*Participant Book,* pages 57–58

Pray: Pray that God will bless you with wisdom and insight.

Day 2:
Reflect: "Every good and perfect gift is from above, coming down from the Father of the heavenly lights, who does not change like shifting shadows" (James 1:17 NIV).

Read: Changing Through Grief—*Participant Book,* pages 58–61

Pray: Pray that you will be a steadfast light through the shifting shadow of grief.

Day 3:
Reflect: "We do not live to ourselves, and we do not die to ourselves" (Romans 14:7 NRSV).

Read: Loneliness—*Participant Book,* pages 62–65

Pray: Pray for your leadership in forming a caring community.

Day 4:

Reflect: "I will never leave you or forsake you" (Hebrews 13:5 NRSV).

Read: Solitude—*Participant Book,* pages 66–69

Pray: Pray for a quiet heart to lead.

Day 5:

Reflect: "I know your works, your toil and your patient endurance" (Revelation 2:2 NRSV).

Read: Rest for Your Soul—*Participant Book,* pages 69–71

Pray: Pray that God will bless your leadership with peace.

Day 6:

Reflect: "Let your steadfast love become my comfort" (Psalm 119:76 NRSV).

Read: Comfort—*Participant Book,* pages 72–75

Pray: Pray for the direction of the Great Comforter as you lead.

Day 7:

Reflect: "This is my comfort in my distress, that your promise gives me life" (Psalm 119:50 NRSV).

Read: Meditate on the poem "The Love of God"—*Participant Book,* pages 75–76

Pray: Pray that God will inspire you to lead the group toward new life.

Session Outline

Greeting (3-4 minutes)

- Begin with a warm word of greeting and inclusion, especially for those who may be new to the group.

- By now you are discovering how best to open the group so that participants engage fully from the start of the session. You continue to assess and understand the emotions of the group, both individually and collectively; you have a better feel for the experience of each participant; you are sensitive and thoughtful in your choice of words.

Opening Prayer (1-2 minutes)
Use the following prayer or adapt the words and spiritual direction to your personal prayer vocabulary.

God, there is pain and heartache as we gather together today in the sanctity of our group. In this time of community apart from the world, we yield our inmost hearts to the care and comfort of the Holy Spirit. We pray that your loving presence will enfold us as we seek your comfort and strength on our journey through grief. Amen.

Video (9-12 minutes)
Play the video for Session 3.

Content Review
(90-minute session: 30 minutes; 60-minute session: 15–18 minutes)

Choose from the following topics according to the time available and the needs of your group.

Changing Through Grief (5–7 minutes)

- Read aloud the following scripture:

  Blessed is the man who perseveres under trial, because when he has stood the test, he will receive the crown of life that God has promised to those who love him. . . . Every good and perfect gift is from above, coming down from the Father of the heavenly lights, who does not change like shifting shadows. (James 1:12, 17 NIV)

- Affirm these points about changing through grief:
  + God is the one constant that does not change.
  + Grief is a "shifting shadow" that changes constantly.
  + Everything changes with the death of a loved one.
  + The "shifting shadow" of grief may feel for a while like a persistent dark cloud.
  + The cloud of grief will one day pass.

- Acknowledge that grief shifts when the business of life forces you to face the reality of the death of your loved one. Discuss examples such as:
  + attending a probate hearing.
  + settling the estate of your loved one.
  + attending to the disposition of things.

- Affirm these points from the video:
  + Grief is both adapting to change and growing into change.
  + Grief can affect you either negatively or positively.
  + Grief can make you:

Stronger	or	Weaker	or	Embittered
More Faithful	or	Disillusioned	or	Spiritually Isolated
More Capable	or	Disabled	or	Dysfunctional
Independent	or	Dependent	or	Helpless
Wiser	or	Stubborn	or	Willful
Deliberate	or	Impulsive	or	Rash

- As time allows, use one or both of these questions modified from the Personal Reflections on page 61 of the *Participant Book* (or others of your choosing) to lead a short discussion about changing through grief:
  + How is your grief changing?
  + How is grief changing you?

Loneliness (5–7 minutes)
- Read aloud the following scripture:

  And after you have suffered for a little while, the God of all grace, who has called you to his eternal glory in Christ, will himself restore, support, strengthen and establish you. (1 Peter 5:10-11 NRSV)

- Affirm these points about loneliness:
  + Loneliness is for many the most painful part of grief.
  + We need to talk about our emotional isolation and express our grief.

- Emphasize these points from the video:
  - ✤ When we express our emotions, we feel better.
  - ✤ We relieve our isolation and loneliness when we reach out to others.
    - – Find someone with whom you may speak freely about your loved one.
    - – Share with others who understand that loneliness is part of grief.
    - – Find an objective listener who will offer professional perspective on your personal issues of grief.

- As time allows, use one or more of these questions modified from the Personal Reflections on page 65 of the *Participant Book* (or others of your choosing) to lead a short discussion about loneliness:
  - ✤ Have you actively sought out and found a confidential grief friend?
  - ✤ If not, how might you do this?
  - ✤ In what ways does the community of a grief group relieve your loneliness?

Solitude (5–7 minutes)
- Read aloud the following scripture:

In quietness and confidence shall be your strength. (Isaiah 30:15 NKJV)

- Affirm these points about solitude:
  - ✤ Solitude and loneliness are not the same.
  - ✤ Solitude is being alone without being lonely.
  - ✤ Sleep is nature's way of ensuring solitude.
  - ✤ Your body and mind are restored through the power of silence.
  - ✤ God is with you in silence and in solitude.
  - ✤ Solitude is not withdrawal from life in monastic silence or antisocial behavior.
  - ✤ Solitude is not a way of life; it is a way of finding life.

- Emphasize the benefits of solitude:
  - ✤ The soul-searching questions of grief are resolved through solitude.
  - ✤ Answers are found in the quiet of the heart.

- Explain how to use solitude for spiritual enrichment:
  - ✤ Listen for God's direction.
  - ✤ Wait in trust for God's answers.

- As time allows, use one or more of these questions modified from Personal Reflections on pages 68–69 of the *Participant Book* (or others of your choosing) to lead a short discussion on solitude:

+ What is the purpose of your life?
+ What is the meaning of your life?
+ How do you find your way in life?

Rest for Your Soul (5–7 minutes)
- Read aloud the following scripture:

"Come to me, all you that are weary and are carrying heavy burdens, and I will give you rest. Take my yoke upon you, and learn from me; for I am gentle and humble in heart, and you will find rest for your souls. For my yoke is easy, and my burden is light." (Matthew 11:28-30 NRSV)

- Affirm these points about rest for your soul in grief:
  + Grief is work.
  + It is physically exhausting to grieve.
  + Grief drains you emotionally.

- Identify with the group what might represent or cause a setback in grief:
  + Illness
  + Infirmity
  + Disability
  + Death of another loved one
  + Holidays
  + Remembrance/anniversary days

- Emphasize that when setbacks occur in grief, you must rest before you try again:
  + Rest your body.
  + Rest your mind.
  + Rest your soul.
  + Rest your spirit.

- Highlight these points from the video:
  + You must lay aside your grief from time to time to rest.
  + One way you rest from grief is by releasing your emotions through tears.
  + You generally feel better after you have had a good cry.
  + Your tears are a form of rest and release.
  + Tears are the expression of the deep feelings that words cannot express.
  + Tears are cleansing; they temporarily wash away some of the emotions of grief.
  + Tears are honest; they allow you to work through the pain of grief.
  + Tears are healing; crying releases tension and physical distress.

- Read aloud Matthew 11:28-29 from *THE MESSAGE*:

  "Are you tired? Worn out? Come to me. Get away with me and you'll recover your life. I'll show you how to take a real rest. Walk with me and work with me—watch how I do it. Learn the unformed rhythms of grace."

  As time allows, ask group participants to share their thoughts about God's invitation to learn "the unforced rhythms of grace" as a way to find rest for the soul.

Comfort (5–7 minutes)
- Read aloud the following scripture:

  Praise be to the God and Father of our Lord Jesus Christ, the Father of compassion and the God of all comfort, who comforts us in all our troubles, so that we can comfort those in any trouble with the comfort we ourselves have received from God. (2 Corinthians 1:3-4 NIV)

- Explain the source of the word comfort: Comfort is from the Latin phrase *com fortis,* meaning "with strength." (Note: As leader, you may find the definitions and other factual information throughout the *Participant Book* helpful in focusing participants on their understanding of grief. Try it as a leadership device; see if it has a centering effect on the group.) Point out the following:
  + To be comforted is to be made strong.
  + In grief, your comfort and strength come from the power and presence of the Holy Spirit, who never leaves you.
  + God is always your Great Comforter.

- Emphasize the nuances of comfort that are a part of grief:
  + We are hurt by our would-be comforters because:
    – Empty words and gestures add to the pain of our grief.
    – We expect others to understand what we are feeling.
    – No one can comfort us to our expectations.
  + We forgive our would-be comforters when we understand that:
    – Only we know the depth of our personal experience of grief.
    – We cannot grieve to the expectations of another.
    – Grief is not a job with a performance standard.
  + We experience the dis-comfort of mental and bodily distress as
    – we struggle to adjust.
    – we struggle to adapt.
    – we struggle to accept the death of our loved one.

✤ We may be truly un-comfort-able when
   – we are unable to receive comfort from others.
   – we are unable or unwilling to be comforted by God.

Discussion and Sharing
(90-minute session: 30–35 minutes; 60-minute session: 15 minutes)

Use this time to engage the group in a discussion of one or more of these questions modified from the Personal Reflections on page 73 in the *Participant Book* (or others of your choosing) to lead a short discussion on comfort.

- How have you been comforted by God?
- Who gives you emotional strength?
- Who offers you unspoken understanding?
- Who inspires you with hope?
- Who is the safe person who responds to your grief with kind, thoughtful intentions?

Summary Statement and Scripture (2 minutes)
Yielding to grief is:
- Acknowledging change
- Relieving loneliness
- Enjoying solitude
- Resting your soul
- Finding comfort

For you have delivered my soul from death, my eyes from tears, my feet from stumbling. (Psalm 116:8 NRSV)

Closing Prayer (1–3 Minutes)
Use the following prayer, offer one of your own, or invite a group member to pray. Or, if your group prefers, allow the group to share prayer concerns and pray for one another.

God, we depart from the sanctuary of our community encouraged and fortified through the power of the Holy Spirit who is our Great Comforter. We are grateful for your abiding presence as we yield to grief and confront the realities of life without our loved ones. We pray that you will accompany us in the days ahead as we rest in the love of your grace. Amen.

SESSION 4: RESPONDING TO GRIEF

Leader Self-care

(A guide for your spiritual preparation prior to Session 4)

My mouth shall speak wisdom; the meditation of my
heart shall be understanding.
Psalm 49:3 NRSV

Day 1:
Reflect: "He gives strength to the weary and increases the power of the weak" (Isaiah 40:29 NIV).

Read: Introduction to Responding to Grief—*Participant Book,* pages 79–80

Pray: Pray that God will use the power of your faith to strengthen the weary.

Day 2:
Reflect: "But you, take courage! Do not let your hands be weak, for your work shall be rewarded" (2 Chronicles 15:7 NRSV).

Read: Making an Effort—*Participant Book,* pages 80–83

Pray: Pray for strong hands and heart as you lead.

Day 3:
Reflect: "Therefore I am content with weaknesses, insults, hardships, persecutions, and calamities for the sake of Christ; for whenever I am weak, then I am strong" (2 Corinthians 12:10 NRSV).

Read: Attitude—*Participant Book,* pages 84–88

Pray: Pray that God will use your strength to transform grief into new life.

Day 4:
Reflect: "My grace is sufficient for you, for power is made perfect in weakness" (2 Corinthians 12:9 NRSV).

Read: Courage—*Participant Book,* pages 89–93

Pray: Pray that your leadership will be blessed by God's all-sufficient grace.

Day 5:
Reflect: For whatever was written in former days was written for our instruction, so that by steadfastness and by the encouragement of the scriptures we might have hope (Romans 15:4).

Read: Victim or Survivor—*Participant Book,* pages 93–94 (through Personal Reflections)

Pray: Pray for the encouragement of the scriptures.

Day 6:
Reflect: "But you, God, see the trouble of the afflicted; you consider their grief and take it in hand. The victims commit themselves to you; you are the helper of the fatherless" (Psalm 10:14 NIV).

Read: Victim or Survivor—*Participant Book,* pages 94–96 (through survival strategies)

Pray: Pray that God will use you to help those afflicted by grief.

Day 7:
Reflect: "By the tender mercy of our God, the dawn from on high will break upon us, to give light to those who sit in darkness and in the shadow of death, to guide our feet into the way of peace" (Luke 1:78-79 NSRV).

Read: Victim or Survivor—*Participant Book,* pages 96–97 (author's reflection to end)

Pray: Pray that God will use you to guide the way into peace.

Session Outline

Greeting (3-4 minutes)
- Begin by expressing gratitude for the faithfulness of those who are, by now, regular participants in the group. You might say, "Thank you for blessing those in our grief group with your participation. Your presence expresses your trust in the safety of our community."
- Always remember to acknowledge those who may be new to the group. Express appreciation for their interest and assure them there is a place for them in the group.
- Encourage those who join the group to read the *Participant Book* to understand the direction and content of missed sessions.
- Be sure that new participants receive a copy of the ground rules (page 36).

Opening Prayer (1–2 minutes)
Use the following prayer or adapt the words and spiritual direction to your personal prayer vocabulary.

God, through your grace we are beginning to understand better our grief. We sometimes hesitate to respond to our grief, especially when we sense what it will take to move toward new life. We are here because we are willing to consider and learn. We pray that you will direct our way through the presence of the Holy Spirit. Amen.

Video (9–12 minutes)
Play the video for Session 4.

Content Review
(90-minute session: 30 minutes; 60-minute session: 15–18 minutes)

Choose from the following topics according to the time available and the needs of your group.

Making an Effort (5–7 minutes)
- Read aloud the following scripture:

  Let us therefore make every effort to do what leads to peace and mutual edification. (Romans 14:19 NIV)

- Explain the meaning of "mutual edification": *the encouragement and comfort we experience when we share our grief within the safe community of a group on a shared journey through grief.*
    - We understand our own grief better when we listen in care to the grief of others.
    - In mutual edification we both give and receive encouragement and comfort.

- Affirm these points from the video:
    - Life takes an effort.
    - Grief demands that we make an effort in order to survive.
    - The assumption of grief is that we are supposed to try to "do" something to help ourselves.

- Review the ways we are challenged by the death of our loved one to try in new, unaccustomed ways to live and be in the world:
    - We try to find where we fit in life without our loved one.
    - We "try on" new ways to live, especially if we are alone for the first time in life.
    - We "try out" new people or routines.
    - We try new experiences.
    - We try to go on with life.

- Affirm some of the beneficial ways we try to make an effort in grief:
    - We use our talents and interests to give to others.
    - We use our unique, God-given gifts and graces to serve others.
    - We use our personal expertise to go beyond ourselves in grief.

- Emphasize this important point to the group:

    If making an effort seems consistently overwhelming, it may be time to seek the help of a confidential, non-judgmental counselor, therapist, or minister who will listen thoughtfully to understand your grief. The guidance of a qualified professional may be critical for understanding your specific, individual issues that can hinder your progress in responding to grief.

- As time allows, use these questions modified from the Personal Reflections on page 83 of the *Participant Book* (or others of your choosing) to lead a short discussion about making an effort in grief:
    - What is difficult about making an effort when you are grieving?
    - What help have you enlisted—or might you enlist—to overcome the inertia of grief?

Attitude (5–7 minutes)
- Read aloud the following scripture:

  Do not conform any longer to the pattern of this world, but be trans-formed by the renewing of your mind. Then you will be able to test and approve what God's will is—his good, pleasing and perfect will. (Romans 12:2 NIV)

- Affirm these points about attitude from the video:
  - ✦ We are not in control of the circumstances of either life or death.
  - ✦ We cannot change what happened.
  - ✦ The only thing we can truly control in grief is our attitude.
  - ✦ Our attitude is a choice.
  - ✦ A positive attitude is shaped by the perspective of our faith.

- Read aloud the following scripture:

  You, however, were taught . . . to put off your old self . . . to be made new in the attitude of your minds; and to put on the new self, created to be like God in true righteousness and holiness. (Ephesians 4:17-18, 22-24 NIV)

- Review some of the discoveries of grief:
  - ✦ We will never again be the same person we once were before the death of our loved one.
  - ✦ We are becoming different persons.
  - ✦ Grief encourages us to become a new self—a different self, a better self.
  - ✦ Our attitude is a vital part of who we are.
  - ✦ Our renewed confidence contributes to a positive attitude.
  - ✦ We honor the memory of our loved one when we choose an attitude of grace.

- As time allows, use these questions modified from Personal Reflections on page 86 of the *Participant Book* (or others of your choosing) to lead a short discussion about our attitude in grief. Point out that our answers reflect our attitude.
  - ✦ Do you choose to live in seclusion, isolated and alone?
  - ✦ Do you choose to blame others, embittered and angry because of the death of your loved one?
  - ✦ Do you choose to torment yourself because you could not save his or her life?
  - ✦ Do you choose to immerse yourself in self-pity, defying the world at large?

- Affirm that the attitude of faith reflects this basic, fundamental truth: *life is worth living.*

Courage (5–7 minutes)
- Read aloud the following scripture:

We are hard pressed on every side, but not crushed; perplexed, but not in despair; persecuted, but not abandoned; struck down, but not destroyed. (2 Corinthians 4: 8-9 NIV)

- Explain the meaning of the word courage: *Courage* is derived from the Latin word *cor,* which means "heart."
  + Courage is your outward response to your inner fear.
  + Courage is your fear turned inside out.
  + Bravery is bold courage inspired by the love of God.
  + Bravery enables us to face difficulty without fear.

- Affirm that faith in the steadfast love of God fortifies our courage:
  + Though your spirit may be hard-pressed by grief, *you are not crushed.*
  + Though you are perplexed by some unanswered question about death, *you do not despair.*
  + Though you perhaps feel struck down for a while by grief, *you are not destroyed.*

- Read aloud the following scripture:

May... God our Father, who loved us and by his grace gave us eternal encouragement and good hope, encourage your hearts and strengthen you in every good deed and word. (2 Thessalonians 2:16-17 NIV)

- Emphasize these points about courage:
  + The best part of courage is *encouragement.*
    - When you share your grief with others who have lost a loved one, you are encouraged by the support of a community.
    - When you receive God's promise of eternal encouragement and good hope, you are blessed with comfort and peace.
    - In courage your strength is renewed.
    - In courage you are resurrected from grief.
    - In courage you are reborn to life.

- As time allows, use these questions modified from the Personal Reflections on page 93 of the *Participant Book* (or others of your choosing) to lead a short discussion about courage:

* What fears do you need to express as courage?
* Who or what gives you encouragement?
* What is your source of spiritual encouragement?

Victim or Survivor (5–7 minutes)
• Read aloud the following scripture:

"For I know the plans I have for you," declares the Lord, "plans to prosper you and not to harm you, plans to give you hope and a future." (Jeremiah 29:11 NIV)

• Read aloud the definition of "victim": A victim is "one who is made to suffer injury, loss, or death."[4]

• Emphasize these points about victimization:
  * With the death of a loved one, you become a victim through no fault or action of your own.
  * Because death is a permanent loss, your life may seem irreparably damaged.
  * A sense of abandonment is a real part of victimization.
    – You may feel abandoned by God or by your loved one.
  * Most people are unprepared to be the victim of death and loss.
  * When you see yourself as a victim, you may feel helpless and powerless.
  * It is easy to feel like a victim when your emotional and physical reserves are depleted by grief.
  * Acknowledge your sense of victimization, but do not give in to it.

• Affirm that choosing to be a survivor is a powerful turning point in grief:
  * You have the choice to survive day to day.
  * You have the choice to survive for life.
  * If you are empowered by the experience of life and death, you want to survive.
  * When you choose survival, you want to be a Survivor—with a capital S.

• Summarize these points:
  * When we choose to be a Survivor:
    – We are thankful for the gift of life.
    – We read for grief understanding and spiritual enrichment.
    – We find both social and spiritual encouragement in a support community.
    – We pray for renewal and personal transformation.
    – We stay connected to the world; it is not waiting on us or for us.

Discussion and Sharing
(90-minute session: 30–35 minutes; 60-minute session: 15 minutes)

Use this time to engage the group in a discussion about responding to grief by choosing to be a Survivor. Highlight several of these survival strategies (*Participant Book*, pages 95–96). Ask those in the group to share their experience of using these strategies to become Survivors:

- Face being alone.
- Name your thoughts and feelings.
- Allow others to see your tears.
- Ask for help—from family, friends, clergy, or a therapist.
- Avoid toxic, angry, or judgmental people and those who want to control.
- Dress and go outside each day.
- Talk to another person each day.
- Move your body; exercise in small ways.
- Eat at least one healthy meal each day.
- Perform only safe tasks that do not exceed your concentration level.
- Avoid excessive use of alcohol and drugs.
- Spend as little money as possible.
- Take care of your health needs because grief impacts the immune system.

Summary Statement and Scripture (2 minutes)
- Death forever changes those who survive.
- Our identity and our worldview change.
- In grief we lose:
  - the one who died
  - the person we were when he or she was alive
  - the assumptions upon which our life was built
  - our vision of the future
- As Survivors, we reestablish our unique identity.
- As Survivors, we claim our place in the mainstream of life.

I will not die, but live.
. . . .
The LORD . . .
has not given me over to death. (Psalm 118:17-18 NASB)

Closing Prayer (1-3 Minutes)
Use the following prayer, offer one of your own, or invite a group member to pray. Or, if your group prefers, allow the group to share prayer concerns and pray for one another.

God, we are challenged because it is so easy in grief to be immobilized by our feelings and emotions. We know that you are at work on our behalf to strengthen us, yet we realize the importance of responding to grief by doing our part. We pray that you will affirm us in our attitude of grace and give us the courage to live boldly in faith as Survivors. Amen.

SESSION 5 – ADJUSTING THROUGH GRIEF

Leader Self-care

(A guide for your spiritual preparation prior to Session 5)

Commit your work to the LORD, and your plans will be established.
Proverbs 16:3 NRSV

Day 1:
Reflect: "Whoever acknowledges me before others, I will also acknowledge before my Father in heaven" (Matthew 10:32 NIV).

Read: Introduction to Adjusting Through Grief—*Participant Book,* pages 101–3

Pray: Pray you will be used to bear witness to God's love and care.

Day 2:
Reflect: "In all your ways acknowledge him, and he will make straight your paths" (Proverbs 3:6 NRSV).

Read: Where Do I Fit in Life?—*Participant Book,* pages 103–6

Pray: Pray that God will make clear to you the path of your leadership.

Day 3:
Reflect: "All this is from God, who reconciled us to himself through Christ, and has given us the ministry of reconciliation; that is, in Christ God was reconciling the world to himself" (2 Corinthians 5:18-19 NRSV).

Read: Gender-specific Grief—*Participant Book,* pages 106–9 (focus on specifics related to men)

Pray: Pray that you will be a reconciler as you minister to those who grieve.

Day 4:

Reflect: "For as in one body we have many members, and not all the members have the same function, so we, who are many, are one body in Christ, and individually we are members one of another" (Romans 12:4-5 NRSV).

Read: Gender-specific Grief—*Participant Book,* pages 106–9 (focus on specifics related to women)

Pray: Pray that participants in your grief group become part of one another.

Day 5:

Reflect: "From everyone who has been given much, much will be demanded; and from the one who has been entrusted with much, much more will be asked" (Luke 12:48 NIV).

Read: Adjustment—*Participant Book,* pages 109–10 (through list of adjustments)

Pray: Pray the community entrusted to your leadership will adjust and grow through grief.

Day 6:

Reflect: "Finally, brothers and sisters, rejoice! Strive for full restoration, encourage one another, be of one mind, live in peace. And the God of love and peace will be with you" (2 Corinthians 13:11 NIV).

Read: Adjustment—*Participant Book,* pages 110–14 (from list to end)

Pray: Pray that your grief group will encourage one another and be of one mind.

Day 7:

Reflect: "My presence will go with you, and I will give you rest" (Exodus 33:14 NRSV).

Read: Acceptance—*Participant Book,* pages 114–17

Pray: Pray that God's presence will be evident through your leadership.

Session Outline

Greeting (3-4 minutes)
- By now you probably have a good feel for the collective spirit of the group. Likely participants are comfortable with one another and look forward to attending the sessions. Because you have worked to create a safe community by honoring the ground rules, members of the group have learned to trust you and rely on your leadership through the journey of grief.

- It may be time to relax and make the greeting an informal time that allows participants to share something uplifting and personal (a family birthday, the birth of a grandchild, a new job or promotion, the decision to move, etc.); this approach may provide positive energy for the session. If you use this idea, be sure to manage the time. Otherwise, you may not have enough time for the content review or other segments of the session.

- Be intentional about including those who may be new to the group. All participants need to feel included.

- Encourage those who are new to the group to read the *Participant Book* for the session content they have missed. Affirm that it is always possible to catch up with the group session content.

Opening Prayer (1–2 minutes)
Use the following prayer or adapt the words and spiritual direction to your personal prayer vocabulary.

God, it stretches our hearts and minds to adjust, especially through the pain of grief. We are at a threshold in our grief because we understand that we must grow in order to live forward. We pray today that you will encourage us in our effort to adjust so that we may claim new life at the end of our journey of grief. Amen.

Video (9–12 minutes)
Play the video for Session 5.

Content Review
(90-minute session: 30 minutes; 60-minute session: 15–18 minutes)

Choose from the following topics according to the time available and the needs of your group.

Where Do I Fit in Life? (5–7 minutes)
- Read aloud the following scripture:

  Do not worry about anything, but in everything by prayer and supplication with thanksgiving let your requests be made known to God. And the peace of God, which surpasses all understanding, will guard your hearts and your minds in Christ Jesus. (Philippians 4:6-7 NRSV)

- Affirm these points from the video:
  - Adjustment moves you away from the past.
  - Adjustment moves you toward new life.
  - Adjustment inspires you to reinvest in the future.
  - Adjustment leads to spiritual growth.

- Emphasize these points in response to the question "Where do I fit in life?"
  - The answer to the question implies, "without my loved one."
  - The struggle to fit in can intensify the heartache of grief.
  - We sometimes see ourselves as "less than" because of the absence of our loved one.
  - Our self-perception may be that we have become "second-class citizens."
  - Moments when we are the "fifth wheel" accentuate our loss and sense of aloneness.

- Remind the group that God understands our anxiety about our new place in the social structure of life:
  - When we grieve, it is sometimes difficult to relax into God's loving care.
  - God promises peace to sustain us as we adjust through grief.
  - When we are at peace,
    - we are restored to a life of full citizenship.
    - we again fit into life with renewed strength.
    - we rediscover our self-confidence.

- As time allows, use one or both of the following questions modified from the Personal Reflections on page 106 of the *Participant Book* (or others of your choosing) to lead a short discussion about "Where do I fit in life?"
  - What are some instances when you have asked, "Where do I fit in life?"
  - How have you grown through your discovery of where you fit in life?

Gender-specific Grief (5–7 minutes)

- Read aloud the following scriptures:

  A *father to the fatherless, a defender of widows, is God in his holy dwelling.* (Psalm 68:5 NIV)

  Jesus wept. (John 11:35 NIV)

- Explain the concept of gender-specific grief:
  - Statistically, women live longer than men do.
  - It is widely presumed that men are strong and do not hurt as much as women.
  - In grief, the emotional needs of a man are often neglected or dismissed.
  - Love is the universal reason that we grieve.
  - Women typically feel comfortable crying, whether tears of sadness or joy.
  - Although men are conditioned not to cry, they should weep when their heart is broken.
  - Jesus wept. There is no greater example for men who grieve.

- Affirm these points about gender-specific grief:
  - For men, the death of a woman may result in social disconnection.
    - The challenge for men is to sustain meaningful contact with others.
    - Isolation, loneliness, and depression are among the most difficult issues of grief for men.
  - Most women have networks for emotional support through family and friends.
    - Especially in marriage, women typically instigate and facilitate relationships.

- As time allows, use these points (from page 108 in the *Participant Book*) to lead a short discussion about gender-specific grief:
  - Some women express helplessness or mild resentment about assuming many responsibilities their husbands may have handled exclusively or primarily, such as:
    - managing finances
    - doing business
    - earning a living
    - having the car serviced
    - keeping the house in repair
    - interacting with service providers

- ✦ Likewise, many practicalities of daily living can be an ongoing struggle for men:
  - – preparing meals
  - – eating alone
  - – doing the laundry
  - – caring for a house that no longer feels like a home without a woman's loving presence

- Read aloud the following scripture:

We...boast in our sufferings, knowing that suffering produces endurance, and endurance produces character, and character produces hope. (Romans 5:3-4 NRSV)

- Affirm these points of faith about gender-specific grief:
  - ✦ We suffer because we have loved and lost a beloved person in our life.
  - ✦ We endure because life demands that we live in the present.
  - ✦ When we endure, we are rewarded with hope.
  - ✦ We dare to hope because,
    - – we believe that God is with us in life.
    - – we believe that God is with us in death.
    - – we believe that God is with us in life beyond death.
    - – we believe that we are not alone.

Adjustment (5–7 minutes)
- Read aloud the following scripture:

But this one thing I do: forgetting what lies behind and straining forward to what lies ahead, I press on toward the goal for the prize of the heavenly call of God in Christ Jesus. (Philippians 3:13-14 NRSV)

- Emphasize these points from the video about ways we must change to adjust through grief:
  - ✦ We adjust to the absence of our loved one.
  - ✦ We adjust to daily life.
  - ✦ We adjust to our new place in the world.
  - ✦ We adjust our social interaction with others.

- Read aloud the following scripture:

Everything old has passed away; see, everything has become new!
(2 Corinthians 5:17 NRSV)

- Affirm these aspects of adjustment:
  - ✤ Growing through grief is the slow work of constant adjustment.
  - ✤ Adjustment is stretching.
    - – We are more resilient than we imagine.
  - ✤ When we adjust, we let go of the physical life that once was.
    - – What lies behind is our history.
    - – We did not die physically when our loved one died.
    - – Our purpose and destiny did not die with the one who is gone.
  - ✤ As we adjust, we hold on to the memories and love and build on the past.
  - ✤ In adjustment, we believe that something does lie ahead.

- Affirm these points from the video:
  - ✤ Adjustment moves us away from the past.
    - – The past is a sacred part of who we will yet become.
  - ✤ Adjustment moves us toward new life.
    - – Our goal lies ahead.
  - ✤ Adjustment inspires us to reinvest in the future.
    - – We reawaken to the joy and possibilities of life.
  - ✤ Adjustment leads to spiritual growth.
    - – We claim the prize of the high calling of God for life.

- As time allows, use one or more of these questions modified from the Personal Reflections on page 114 of the *Participant Book* (or others of your choosing) to lead a short discussion about adjustment:
  - ✤ What are the challenges of adjustment for you?
  - ✤ What crises of self-esteem are you experiencing?
  - ✤ How do you hold on and let go at the same time?

Acceptance (5–7 minutes)
- Read aloud the following scripture:

  We know that in everything God works for good with those who love him, who are called according to his purpose. (Romans 8:28 RSV)

- Affirm these points about acceptance:
  - ✤ Acceptance is the emotional maturing of our adjustment to life as it is becoming.
  - ✤ When adjustment becomes the norm, we are on the way to acceptance.
    - – We accept that our loved one is physically gone.
    - – We acknowledge that our loss is permanent.
    - – We know that the outcome cannot be changed.
    - – We realize that the love of the one lost lives within us forever.
  - ✤ We work at acceptance.

- Emphasize the spiritual aspects of acceptance in the video:
  - It is normal to question how the death of our loved one can possibly be for good in our life.
  - Even though we do not understand the "why" of death, we believe that God is at work on our behalf for good.
  - The case for acceptance lies within the prepositions:
    - *God is here in everything.*
      God has not ordained our loss and sorrow.
      God meets us at our place of brokenness.
    - *God works for good.*
      God uses grief to teach us more of God's faithfulness and steadfast love.
      God uses that which has changed our life to promote deeper, more profound faith.
    - *God works with us.*
      We are called according to God's purpose.
      We have faith in God's plan for our life.
      God works *with* us to shape a life of meaning and purpose.

Discussion and Sharing
(90-minute session: 30–35 minutes; 60-minute session: 15 minutes)

Use this time to engage the group in a discussion about adjusting through grief by using these questions modified from the Personal Reflections on page 117 in the *Participant Book* (or others of your choosing):
- What is your experience of God's good at work in your life?
- Have you reached the moment of acceptance? If so, when did it happen?
- Have you consciously acknowledged that you are no longer actively grieving?
- What are the signs of acceptance for you—or what do you think they will be?

Summary Statement and Scripture (2 minutes)
The events of our physical, emotional, and spiritual acceptance of death do not occur simultaneously.
- We arrive at acceptance when we,
  - deconstruct our subconscious walls of self-protection
  - live again in open, free exchange with others and the world

- Our thoughts determine who we are and how we live.
  - When we listen, we hear what our heart says to us after the death of our loved one.
  - Our words speak to us of that which dwells deep within.
    - Acceptance speaks peace.

    – Acceptance speaks love.
    – Acceptance speaks gratitude for the gift of life.

I am the resurrection and the life. He who believes in me, though he die, yet shall he live. And whoever lives and believes in me shall never die. (John 11:25-26 RSV)

Closing Prayer (1–3 Minutes)

Use the following prayer, offer one of your own, or invite a group member to pray. Or, if your group prefers, allow the group to share prayer concerns and pray for one another.

God, as we adjust through grief we pray that we may claim the victory of acceptance in the assurance of faith that there is life beyond death. We believe that you are the resurrection and life. We know that in Christ we will be reunited with the one we have loved and lost in death who lives now in eternity with you. Through your grace may we accept the promise of new life. Amen.

SESSION 6 – MOVING FORWARD IN GRIEF

Leader Self-care

(A guide for your spiritual preparation prior to Session 6)

I will instruct you and teach you the way you should go;
I will counsel you with my eye upon you.
Psalm 32:8 NRSV

Day 1:
Reflect: "Wait for the LORD; be strong, and let your heart take courage; wait for the LORD!" (Psalm 27:14 NRSV).

Read: Introduction to Moving Forward in Grief—*Participant Book,* pages 121–22

Pray: Pray that God will encourage your heart as you lead.

Day 2:
Reflect: "I bless the LORD who gives me counsel; in the night also my heart instructs me" (Psalm 17:7 NRSV).

Read: How Long Does Grief Last—*Participant Book,* pages 122–24

Pray: Pray that your leadership will reflect God's counsel and wisdom.

Day 3:
Reflect: "Then you shall call, and the LORD will answer; you shall cry for help, and he will say, Here I am" (Isaiah 58:9a NRSV).

Read: Healing—*Participant Book,* pages 125–27

Pray: Pray that you will hear God's voice as you lead.

Day 4:
Reflect: "I will heal my people and will let them enjoy abundant peace and security" (Jeremiah 33:6 NIV).

Read: Review Healing—*Participant Book,* pages 125–27

Pray: Pray that God will use your leadership in the healing of those who grieve.

Day 5:
Reflect: "Happy are those who make the LORD their trust" (Psalm 40:4 NRSV).

Read: Happiness—*Participant Book,* pages 128–30

Pray: Pray that your trust in God inspires your leadership.

Day 6:
Reflect: "For God alone my soul waits in silence, for my hope is from him" (Psalm 62:5 NRSV).

Read: Hope—*Participant Book,* pages 131–32

Pray: Pray that silence instructs you in the hope of God.

Day 7:
Reflect: Now hope that is seen is not hope. For who hopes for what is seen? But if we hope for what we do not see, we wait for it with patience" (Romans 8:24-25 NRSV).

Read: Hope—*Participant Book,* pages 133–35

Pray: Pray for patience to learn more of hope.

Session Outline

Greeting (3-4 minutes)
- Although no two people are at exactly the same place at any time on the journey of grief, by now likely you have identified within the group points of commonality among the participants that you are using to direct your leadership.

- Use one of the topics you have found to be a common objective of most participants to support your greeting. For example, you might say, "Thank you again today for your presence, which continues to enrich our group. Although we're not all at the same place on our journey of grief, over the past few sessions we have all expressed a desire to move forward in our grief. Helping each other is the blessing of our community. Let's see how we can encourage one another again today to move the next step forward."

- If there are those who are new to the group, take a moment to make them feel included. However, it is important to continue to lead for the greater good. Remember that it is not necessary for you to stop and devote session time to "catching up" one or more individuals (see Leader Support page 35). Perhaps you can quickly summarize the previous sessions in 1–2 minutes for those who are new.

- Encourage any new members of the group to read the *Participant Book* for the session content they have missed.

Opening Prayer (1–2 minutes)
Use the following prayer or adapt the words and spiritual direction to your personal prayer vocabulary.

God, we dare to consider moving forward in grief even though we still have questions and doubts about life. At times we waver between the past and the present, but we believe that there is a future for us beyond our grief. We long to be healed; we desire a return to happiness and joy. We pray that through the Holy Spirit you will fill us with hope. Amen.

Video (9-12 minutes)
Play the video for Session 6.

Content Review
(90-minute session: 30 minutes; 60-minute session: 15–18 minutes)

Choose from the following topics according to the time available and the needs of your group.

How Long Does Grief Last? (5–7 minutes)
- Read aloud the following scripture:

  "A little while, and you will no longer see me, and again a little while, and you will see me." (John 16:19 NRSV)

- Affirm these points about the scripture:
  - Jesus tells us that we will grieve "for a little while."
  - "A little while" is not forever.
  - We are assured that we will be restored and made whole again.

- Explain these points about moving forward in grief:
  - No one grieves in the same way or at the same pace.
  - Grief does not follow the calendar.
  - Grief comes and it goes.
  - Grief will not be rushed.
  - Grief usually lasts longer than most expect.

- Emphasize these points from the video:
  - When and how grief begins may affect how long grief lasts.
  - You grieve as long as you grieve.
  - Grief lasts as long as it lasts.
  - Grief does not last forever.

- As time allows, lead a short discussion about the "shelf life" of grief (see pages 122–24 of the *Participant Book*).

Healing (5–7 minutes)
- Read aloud the following scripture:

  He heals the brokenhearted, and binds up their wounds. (Psalm 147:3 NRSV)

- Affirm these points from the video:
  - We question whether we want to be healed from grief.
  - We question if we will heal from grief.
  - We question how long it will take to heal from grief.

- We question whether we could be satisfied to live with a permanently broken heart.
- We affirm with the psalmist there is healing from grief.

- Explain the ways in which death wounds the human soul and spirit:
  - The greater the love for a loved one, the larger and deeper the wound.
    - For some, the wound is so deep that healing sometimes seems almost impossible.
    - For others, the wound is less severe.
  - The wounds of our grief must be taken seriously.
    - Our wound may be due to slow leave-taking from our loved one after months or years of chronic illness.
    - Our wound may be a gaping injury in need of immediate, acute care because of a sudden or tragic death.
  - In faith we believe that all wounds of the soul can be healed.

- Affirm these points about healing:
  - Healing is the gradual process of becoming whole or sound.
  - Spiritual and emotional healing from grief is best described as recovery.
  - We are recovering if we are finding satisfaction again in life.
  - We are recovering when we hear ourselves say positively and affirmatively:
    - "I am better."
    - "I want to live."
    - "Life is good."
  - When we are healed from grief, we have a scar in our soul to remind us of our grief.
    - Scar tissue becomes the strongest part of the human body.
    - As we slowly heal from grief, we become strongest in our broken places.
    - Our scar is the spiritual and emotional symbol of our most acute pain.
  - Our broken heart is healed by the grace of God, the Great Physician.

- As time allows, use one or more of these questions modified from Personal Reflections on page 127 of the *Participant Book* (or others of your choosing) to lead a short discussion about healing:
  - How long does it take to heal?
  - How long do you think it will take for you to heal?
  - When will you know that you are healed?
  - How will you know that you are healed?

Happiness (5–7 minutes)
- Read aloud the following scripture:

  "Blessed are those who mourn, for they will be comforted." (Matthew 5:4 NRSV)

- Explain this about the scripture, which is the fourth beatitude or "declaration of blessedness" from the Sermon on the Mount in Matthew 5:1-12:
  + There is a connection between mourning, blessedness, and happiness.
    – The word *beatitude* comes from Latin roots that mean "happy," "blessed," or "to make happy."
    – We are assured that because we mourn, we will be *blessed* or *happy*.
  + We struggle to reconcile blessedness with mourning, and happiness with grief.
  + Our best perspective may be this:
    – Because we mourn, we are comforted.
    – When we are comforted, we are blessed.
  + Grief insists that we mourn before we are blessed with authentic comfort and happiness.

- Affirm these points about happiness:
  + Happiness is not a random state of mind or being.
  + Happiness is a choice we make for the rest of our life.
  + Happiness comes from within; it happens inside your heart.
  + A life of service is the secret to happiness.
  + Happiness is a sign we are moving forward in grief.
  + Happiness is spiritual joy.

- As time allows, use these questions (or others of your choosing) to lead a short discussion about happiness (see page 129 of the *Participant Book*):
  + What makes you happy?
  + When are you happy?
  + Do you have the inner stability to live a life of sustained happiness? Why or why not?
  + Are you moving forward in grief toward joy?

Hope (5–7 minutes)
- Read aloud the following scripture:

But this I call to mind, and therefore I have hope: The steadfast love of the LORD never ceases; his mercies never come to an end; they are new every morning; great is your faithfulness. "The Lord is my portion," says my soul, "therefore I will hope in him." (Lamentations 3:21-24 ESV)

- Affirm these points from the video:
    + Hope is not naïve optimism.
    + Hope is not wishful thinking.
    + Hope is not a positive attitude.
    + Hope is not a passive wish or dream.

- Emphasize these points about hope in grief:
    + Grief assaults our hope.
    + Without hope, it is easy to despair.
    + When you hope you do not despair.
    + Hope is more than an emotion.
    + It is the nature of the human heart to hope.
    + The steady upward trajectory of grief is hope.
    + Hope is our fear defeated.

- Affirm these points about the spiritual qualities of hope:
    + We hope because we are divinely created human beings.
    + In faith there is always hope in God.
    + The faith of grief inspires us to trust that there is a future through the grace of God.
    + The hope of grief is confidence in the divine plan of a loving, caring God.
    + We hope because we have faith.

- Make these points about prayer:
    + The most active form of our hope is expressed in prayer.
    + In prayer we entrust the most fervent hopes of our heart to God.
    + We pray because we desire restoration to life.
    + We pray for strength because we are changed by the experience of grief.
    + We pray for hope.
    + We pray in hope.
    + In prayer we affirm the present and live in hope.

- Read aloud the following scripture:

And hope does not disappoint us because God has poured out his love into our hearts through the Holy Spirit. (Romans 5:5 NRSV)

- Affirm these points about hope:
  - ✤ Hope is sacred evidence of expectancy, patience, trust, and faith.
  - ✤ What God has done illuminates what God will do.
  - ✤ Hope does not rely on our own aspirations but on God.
  - ✤ We hope for the future because the future belongs to God.
  - ✤ In God, the best is yet to be.

Discussion and Sharing
(90-minute session: 30–35 minutes; 60-minute session: 15 minutes)

Use this time to engage the group in a discussion about hope using these questions modified from the Personal Reflections on page 135 in the *Participant Book* (or others of your choosing):
- What do you hope for in life?
- What inspires your hope?
- Is your hope based in reality or fantasy?
- Do you have the spiritual resolve to hope again for a life that is full, even without your loved one?

Summary Statement and Scripture (2 minutes)
- As we move forward in grief:
  - ✤ We believe there is a future.
  - ✤ We have hope for the future.
  - ✤ We entertain the idea of joy.
  - ✤ We reach out to life.

May the God of hope fill you with all joy and peace as you trust in him, so that you may overflow with hope by the power of the Holy Spirit. (Romans 15:13 NIV)

Closing Prayer (1–3 Minutes)
Use the following prayer, offer one of your own, or invite a group member to pray. Or, if your group prefers, allow the group to share prayer concerns and pray for one another.

God, we leave today more confident about life because of the promises of our faith. We pray that you will reawaken us fully to the glory of life through your eternal love and joy. As we depart from our grief community, we join with the psalmist in praise and prayer, "May your unfailing love rest upon us, O Lord, even as we put our hope in you" (Psalm 33:22 NIV). Amen.

SESSION 7 – GROWING SPIRITUALLY THROUGH GRIEF

Leader Self-care

(A guide for your spiritual preparation prior to Session 7)

Don't hesitate to be enthusiastic—be on fire in the Spirit as you serve the Lord!
Romans 12:11 CEB

Day 1:
Reflect: "O LORD, you are my God; I will exalt you and praise your name, for in perfect faithfulness you have done marvelous things, things planned long ago (Isaiah 25:1 NIV).

Read: Introduction to Growing Spiritually Through Grief—*Participant Book,* pages 139–42

Pray: Pray that your leadership will inspire spiritual growth.

Day 2:
Reflect: "Your love, O LORD, reaches to the heavens, your faithfulness to the skies" (Psalm 36:5 NIV).

Read: The Faithfulness of God—*Participant Book,* pages 142–44 (through Deuteronomy 33:27)

Pray: Pray for understanding of the expanse of God's faithfulness.

Day 3:
Reflect: "The steadfast love of the LORD never ceases, his mercies never come to an end; they are new every morning; great is your faithfulness" (Lamentations 3:22-23 NRSV).

Read: The Faithfulness of God—*Participant Book,* pages 144–46 (author's reflection to end)

Pray: Pray that you will be refreshed by God's steadfast love.

Day 4:
Reflect: "Go through, go through the gates, prepare the way for the people; build up, build up the highway, clear it of stones" (Isaiah 62:10 NRSV).

Read: Reconstruction—*Participant Book,* pages 146–47 (through Personal Reflections)

Pray: Pray that your leadership will clear the way for new life.

Day 5:
Reflect: "For everything there is a season, and a time for every matter under heaven: a time to be born, and a time to die; . . . a time to break down, and a time to build up." (Ecclesiastes 3:1-3 NRSV)

Read: Reconstruction—*Participant Book,* pages 148–49 (principles of construction to end)

Pray: Pray that God will use you to build up the faith of the group.

Day 6:
Reflect: "I know what it is to be in need, and I know what it is to have plenty. I have learned the secret of being content in any and every situation, whether well fed or hungry, whether living in plenty or in want" (Philippians 4:12 NIV).

Read: Choose Life—*Participant Book,* pages 149–52

Pray: Pray that you will be blessed with contentment as you lead.

Day 7:
Reflect: "My soul is satisfied as with a rich feast, and my mouth praises you with joyful lips . . . for you have been my help, and in the shadow of your wings I sing for joy"(Psalm 63:5, 7 NRSV).

Read: Review Choose Life—*Participant Book,* pages 149–52

Pray: Pray that words from your lips will be joyful and feed the souls in your group.

Session Outline

Greeting (3-4 minutes)
- As you near the conclusion of the structured grief program, you may want to use the greeting time to ask each participant to express to another member of the group how his or her presence and/or sharing is a blessing.

- If you use this approach, ensure that each person is addressed with a positive affirmation.

- End the greeting with a word of affirmation for the group as a community.

Opening Prayer (1–2 minutes)
Use the following prayer or adapt the words and spiritual direction to your personal prayer vocabulary.

God, we are thankful for the many ways in which we see and feel that you are growing us spiritually through our grief. We are grateful for your patience, for your understanding of our emotions, and for your faithfulness to our broken hearts. We pray that you will continue to transform our sorrow into joy as we move from darkness into the light of new life. Amen.

Video (9–12 minutes)
Play the video for Session 7.

Content Review
(90-minute session: 30 minutes; 60-minute session: 15–18 minutes)

Choose from the following topics according to the time available and the needs of your group.

The Faithfulness of God (6-10 minutes)
- Read aloud the following scripture:

  Give thanks to him, bless his name. For the Lord is good; his steadfast love endures forever, and his faithfulness to all generations. (Psalm 100: 4-5 NRSV)

- Affirm these points from the video:
  - ✦ God is faithful.
  - ✦ God's goodness and steadfast love never fail you.
  - ✦ God's faithfulness sustains you on your journey through grief.

- Emphasize how grief leads to our spiritual growth:
  - ✦ We are forced by grief to take an active role in our own well-being.
  - ✦ This occurs constantly and on many levels.
  - ✦ At times it may seem overwhelming.
    - – We choose our attitude about what has happened to change our life.
    - – We adapt ourselves to life.
    - – We adjust to life as it is becoming.
    - – We learn to accept that which we cannot change.
  - ✦ All the while we are growing—mentally, emotionally, and spiritually.

- As time allows, use one or more of the following points to lead a discussion about the faithfulness of God (see also *Participant Book,* page 143):
  - ✦ God is with you through the loneliness of grief.
  - ✦ God strengthens you when you are weak.
  - ✦ God encourages you when you despair.
  - ✦ God speaks wisdom in the quiet of your heart.
  - ✦ God provides for your needs.
  - ✦ God watches over you with love and care.
  - ✦ God uses others to minister to you in grief.
  - ✦ God encourages you through the Holy Spirit.

- End this topic with a short discussion of the question "What personal evidence of God's faithfulness to you is growing you spiritually through grief?" (See the similar question in Personal Reflections on page 146 in the *Participant Book.*)

Reconstruction (6–10 minutes)
- Read aloud the following scripture:

*Unless the L*ord *builds the house, those who build it labor in vain.* (Psalm 127:1 NRSV)

- Affirm these points from the video:
  - ✦ We grow spiritually through grief when we commit to rebuilding our lives.
  - ✦ We are required to remodel and/or rebuild our life when our loved one dies.

* ✦ Our personal reconstruction project is both stimulating and creative.
* ✦ Rebuilding a life without our loved one stretches both our mind and heart.
* ✦ As we rebuild, we consider the possibilities for new life.

* Read aloud the following scripture:

The rain came down, the streams rose, and the winds blew and beat against that house; yet it did not fall, because it had its foundation on the rock. (Matthew 7:25 NIV)

* Emphasize these points about reconstruction:
    * ✦ The most essential part of any structure is a solid foundation.
        * – When life is deconstructed by death, our structure may seem near total collapse.
        * – Our life is built on God, the one foundation that never fails.
        * – When loss and sorrow quake the bedrock of our soul, we are secure.
        * – We build on the faithful, steadfast love of God.

* Use these points from the video to lead a discussion about reconstruction (see also *Participant Book,* pages 148–49):
    * ✦ There is a plan to follow.
        * – For every building project there is a design.
    * ✦ Construction is hard work.
        * – Strength, aptitude, and commitment are required to complete the job.
    * ✦ Construction is handwork.
        * – The hands of a laborer show the wear and tear of hard use.
    * ✦ Construction requires tools.
        * – We hammer, unscrew, saw off, level, and realign to reconstruct our life.
    * ✦ Reconstruction is the work of self-nurture.
        * – Honoring our body with proper care ensures a sound structure.
    * ✦ Reconstruction is the work of faith.
        * – We build on the Rock.

* Affirm these spiritual points:
    * ✦ Faith inspires us to do the hard work of reconstruction in grief.
    * ✦ We grow spiritually as we rebuild our lives in partnership with God.

* As time allows, lead a short discussion using one or more of these questions modified from the Personal Reflections on page 147 in the *Participant Book* (or others of your choosing):

+ Do you want to expend the effort for an unknown future?
+ Do you have the stamina, discipline, and will to complete personal reconstruction?
+ Are you influenced by the judgment and opinion of others as you seek to rebuild a new life of your own design?
+ Do you have the determination to work at your own pace, with completion at some unknown time, sooner or later?

Choose Life (6–10 minutes)
- Read aloud the following scripture:

Now choose life, so that you and your children may live and that you may love the LORD your God, listen to his voice, and hold fast to him. For the LORD is your life. (Deuteronomy 30:19-20 NIV)

- Affirm these points from the video:
  + We make hundreds of choices each day.
  + *Choice* means that there are options:
    – We decide between things.
    – We decide among things.
    – We decide about things.
  + Our choices often reflect our attitude toward both life and death because of our grief.
  + We may decide not to choose.
  + We choose to do nothing.
    – If we have mental, emotional, or spiritual inertia, we may be temporarily stuck in grief.
    – If we find that we do not want to be helped in or through our grief, it may be time to seek professional guidance.
  + We may decide to wait and see before we choose and try.
    – When we are ready, our choice to move forward is intuitive as we decide affirmatively to choose life.
    – This choice affirms our spiritual growth through grief.
  + The highest and best choice in grief is to live in faith.
    – We trust that God has a plan for our future.
    – We rejoin life in the fullness for which God created us.
    – When we choose to move forward in grief, we plan for the future by making wise, informed decisions about life.
  + We choose a life of selfless service.
    – When we serve others in love, we give ourselves.

- Read aloud the following scripture:

Choose this day whom you will serve; . . . but as for me and my household, we will serve the Lord. (Joshua 24:15 NRSV)

- Affirm that when we choose life, we are only a small step away from joy:
  - ❖ Grief turns to joy when life blossoms in unexpected ways.
  - ❖ Grief turns to joy in moments that celebrate the life of your loved one.
  - ❖ Grief turns to joy with the birth of a child or grandchild.
  - ❖ Grief turns to joy with a new companion for the rest of life's journey.
  - ❖ Grief will turn to joy when at last you are reunited with the one whose loss you have grieved.

- Make these points about joy:
  - ❖ Joy is the enrichment of love.
  - ❖ Joy is the uplifting of peace.
  - ❖ Joy is the benefit of trust.
  - ❖ Joy is the radiance of hope.
  - ❖ Joy is the light of faith.
  - ❖ Joy is the substance of our soul.
  - ❖ Joy is the balance of peace and hope in our heart.
  - ❖ Joy is in the moment when we want to live again.
  - ❖ Joy is the ultimate quest of our grief journey.

Discussion and Sharing
(90-minute session: 30–35 minutes; 60-minute session: 15 minutes)

Use this time to engage the group in a discussion about the video's content on re-learning joy; point out that this might be thought of as "re-joicing." Highlight the following points to emphasize that it may require spiritual focus to consciously reclaim joy in life:

- Consider joy.
  - ❖ Think of a happiness that is deep and spiritual.
- Practice joy.
  - ❖ Celebrate the life of your loved one.
- Make joy a habit.
  - ❖ Be joyful each day in God.
- Remember the glory of joy.
  - ❖ Awaken to life as it blossoms with hope for the future.
- Recall the deep spiritual satisfaction of joy.
  - ❖ Rejoice in the Lord always.

- Look for joy.
  - ✤ Be patient.
  - ✤ Wait on the Lord.

Summary Statement and Scripture (2 minutes)
- When joy calls us to the other side of grief, we rediscover the energy of joy in our life:
  - ✤ We live with renewed enthusiasm and engagement.
  - ✤ We allow love to flood our life again with rich, unimaginable blessing.
  - ✤ We greet the new day of the rest of our life with expectation and hope.

You have turned my mourning into dancing; you have taken off my sackcloth and clothed me with joy, so that my soul may praise you and not be silent. O LORD my God, I will give thanks to you forever. (Psalm 30:11-12 NRSV)

Closing Prayer (1–3 Minutes)
Use the following prayer, offer one of your own, or invite a group member to pray. Or, if your group prefers, allow the group to share prayer concerns and pray for one another.

God, at this crossroad on our grief journey, we rest in the assurance that you are a faithful God whose promises are eternal. We pray for your guidance as we rebuild our lives on the firm foundation of you as our Rock. As we leave our community today, inspire our hearts to choose life and relearn the glory of our joy in you. Amen.

SESSION 8 – LIVING BEYOND GRIEF

Leader Self-care

(A guide for your spiritual preparation prior to Session 8)

Remember your leaders, those who spoke the word of God to you; consider the outcome of their way of life, and imitate their faith.
Hebrews 13:7 NRSV

Day 1:
Reflect: "The LORD is good to all, and his compassion is over all that he has made" (Psalm 145:9 NRSV).

Read: Introduction to Living Beyond Grief—*Participant Book,* page 155–56

Pray: Pray that your leadership reflects God's goodness.

Day 2:
Reflect: "By day the LORD commands his steadfast love, and at night his song is with me, a prayer to the God of my life" (Psalm 42:8 NRSV).

Read: Durable Love—*Participant Book,* pages 156–58

Pray: Pray that you will hear God's song.

Day 3:
Reflect: "How precious is your steadfast love, O God!" (Psalm 36:7 NRSV).

Read: Review Durable Love—*Participant Book,* pages 156–58

Pray: Pray that your leadership inspires understanding of God's steadfast love.

Day 4:
Reflect: "For your steadfast love is before my eyes, and I walk in faithfulness to you"(Psalm 26:3 NRSV).

Read: Gifts of Your Spirit: A Lasting Legacy—*Participant Book,* pages 158–60 (through Personal Reflections)

Pray: Pray that your leadership is a walk in faithfulness.

Day 5:
Reflect: "In this is love, not that we loved God but that he loved us" (1 John 4:10 NRSV).

Read: Gifts of Your Spirit: A Lasting Legacy—*Participant Book,* pages 160–64 (bottom of page 160 through Love, Goodness, Service)

Pray: Pray that God's love guides your leadership.

Day 6:
Reflect: "For the kingdom of God is not food and drink but righteousness and peace and joy in the Holy Spirit" (Romans 14:17 NRSV).

Read: Gifts of Your Spirit: A Lasting Legacy—*Participant Book,* pages 164–67 (Faith, Compassion, Hope)

Pray: Pray that the Holy Spirit will encourage your leadership with peace and joy.

Day 7:
Reflect: "Precious in the sight of the LORD is the death of his faithful ones" (Psalm 116:15 NRSV).

Read: Review Gifts of Your Spirit–A Lasting Legacy—*Participant Book,* pages 158–67

Pray: Pray that your leadership will bear the fruit of the Spirit.

Session Outline

Greeting (3-4 minutes)
- If this is the last session that the group will meet, you may want to use this time to ask participants to share how the community has blessed their grief. Or you might ask how their grief has been transformed by being in a group with others who understand their grief. (For example, relief from isolation and loneliness, encouragement, hope, etc.)

- End the greeting with a word of personal appreciation for the trust and faithfulness of the group.

- Assure participants that sharing their grief has created an emotional and spiritual bond that will endure long after the group sessions are over.

Opening Prayer (1–2 minutes)

Use the following prayer or adapt the words and spiritual direction to your personal prayer vocabulary.

God, today we celebrate because together we have shared the journey of grief. We are grateful for your steadfast love and faithfulness to us every step of the way. Through your grace, we are ready to walk forward, into the light of life beyond grief. We pray that you will guide us in your peace as we move toward the end of our journey. Amen.

Video (9–12 minutes)
Play the video for Session 8.

Content Review
(90-minute session: 30 minutes; 60-minute session: 15–18 minutes)

Choose from the following topics according to the time available and the needs of your group.

Durable Love (8–15 minutes)
- Read aloud the following scripture:

  Love knows no limit to its endurance, no end to its trust, no fading of its hope; it can outlast anything. It is, in fact, the one thing that still stands when all else has fallen. (1 Corinthians 13:7-8 JBP)

- Affirm these points from the video:
  - ❖ The time and space we shared with our loved one is both sacred and eternal.
    - – It will always be part of who we are.
    - – No one can take it away.
    - – Nothing can destroy it.
  - ❖ Our loved one will always love us.
    - – His or her love for us transcends the event of death.
  - ❖ Love can outlast anything.
    - – Love is the one thing that still stands when all else has fallen.

- Read aloud the following scripture:

  So we have known and believe the love that God has for us. God is love, and those who abide in love abide in God, and God abides in them. (1 John 4:16 NRSV)

- Emphasize these points about the scripture:
  - ❖ We know that God is love.
  - ❖ We know that God ordains love.
  - ❖ We are made whole by the absolute power of God's love.
  - ❖ God's grace is love at work in our life.

- Affirm these points about the legacy of our love:
  - ❖ Our legacy of love is part of who we are.
  - ❖ The love we shared in this life will never die.
    - – We are separated from our loved one in body, but not in heart.
    - – Death cannot destroy love.
    - – Love is eternal.
  - ❖ Our shared love lives on when we invest it in others.
  - ❖ When we give away our love, it grows.

- As time allows, use these questions modified from the Personal Reflections on page 158 of the *Participant Book* (or others of your choosing) to lead a short discussion about durable love:
  - ❖ What do you do with your earthly, mortal love?
  - ❖ How do you care for it?
  - ❖ How do you nurture it?
  - ❖ How do you spend it?

Gifts of Your Spirit: A Lasting Legacy (8–15 minutes)
- Read aloud the following scripture:

We brought absolutely nothing with us when we entered this world and we can be sure we shall take absolutely nothing with us when we leave it. (1 Timothy 6:7-8 JBP)

- Affirm these points from the video:
  - Our personal legacy is not necessarily one of material possessions or wealth.
  - No amount of money or property can substitute for gifts of our spirit to those we love.
    - We cannot take the things of this world with us when we die.
    - When we assess our values, we determine the worth of our lasting legacy.
  - Stewardship is managing our God-given resources to benefit and endow others.
  - Generosity energizes our enjoyment of life in the present.
  - A well-edited life gives us:
    - peace of mind
    - peace of heart
    - peace of soul
  - Our lasting legacy is much more than the things of this world.

- As time allows, use one or more of these questions modified from the Personal Reflections on page 160 of the *Participant Book* (or others of your choosing) to lead a short discussion about stewardship:
  - Do you think you are realistic about the disposition of the things of this world? Why or why not?
  - What are you hanging on to that you need to give away?
  - What provisions are you making for this part of your legacy so that it does not overshadow your lasting spiritual legacy?

- Read aloud the following scripture:

But the fruit of the Spirit is love, joy, peace, patience, kindness, goodness, faithfulness, gentleness and self-control. (Galatians 5.22-23 NIV)

- Emphasize these points in reference to the scripture:
  - The gifts of our spirit are born of the fruit of the Spirit—the Holy Spirit.
  - The gifts of our spirit are our spiritual qualities that live on in others after we die.
  - The gifts of our spirit are our living endowment to those we love.

- Affirm these points from the video:
  - If we could give but one gift, the greatest would be *love*.

+ A life of authentic *goodness* inspires and enriches others by our example.
+ A heart of *service* lives on in others forever.
+ Those we love learn best about our *faith* by how we live.
+ We teach *compassion* to those we love by our spiritual response to life's trials and tragedies.
+ We endow those we love with the glory of *hope* when we live in expectancy and trust.

• As time allows, use one or more of these questions modified from the Personal Reflections on page 165 of the *Participant Book* (or others of your choosing) to lead a short discussion about the character of our spiritual estate:
  + How would you describe who you are in your inmost heart?
  + What are some of the qualities of your soul?
  + How would you describe yourself?
  + What three words would you use to characterize who you are?
  + Do you think that others would use the same words? Why or why not?
  + Do you believe in one way yet live in another?

Discussion and Sharing
(90-minute session: 30–35 minutes; 60-minute session: 15 minutes)

Use this time to engage the group in a discussion about the qualities of our lasting legacy using one or more of these questions modified from the Personal Reflections on page 166 of the *Participant Book* (or others of your choosing):
• What are your qualities that you see reflected in those you love?
• What words would you use to describe your best qualities, those you would like to endow?
• What words would you use to describe the qualities you would not like to see reflected in others?
• Beyond your family, where do you see a reflection of your investment in others or in institutions?
• Where have you planted the seeds that will become your lasting legacy?
• What would you want to be said of you at your funeral or memorial/celebration of life service?
• What words describe how you would like others to remember you?

Summary Statement and Scripture (2 minutes)
• Our greatest legacy to others is the spiritual maturity we acquire on the journey of grief:

+ We have survived the death of our loved one.
+ Ultimately we conquer the experience of grief.
+ We thank God that there is life beyond the broken heart.
+ We thank God for the victory over death.

By the tender mercy of our God, the dawn from on high will break upon us, to give light to those who sit in darkness and in the shadow of death, to guide our feet into the way of peace. (Luke 1:78-79 NSRV)

Closing Prayer (1–3 Minutes)

Use the following prayer, offer one of your own, or invite a group member to pray. Or, if your group prefers, allow the group to share prayer concerns and pray for one another.

God, we are grateful for the hope and promise of life beyond our grief. We join hearts in the sacred bond of our grief community and offer this prayer today as a benediction to our grief journey: "We have come this far by faith, and we will continue to walk with our hand in yours wherever you lead us." Amen.

SUPPLEMENT

SESSION 9 – GRIEF AT THE HOLIDAYS

(1-3 sessions)

How to Use This Material

- It is effective to use "Grief at the Holidays" during November and December. Enough material is provided for three sessions, if desired. If you have one session before Thanksgiving and two sessions before Christmas, the group has continuous support throughout the holiday season.

- Each of the three topics in chapter 9 of the *Participant Book* is relatively short. A session on each topic—The Season, The Experience, The Light—allows the group time for rich, cathartic conversation about the emotions of grief at the holiday season.

- If you plan to have three sessions, use the short meditations in *Beyond the Broken Heart: Daily Devotions for Your Grief Journey* (see the section Grief Is Celebration pages 189–207)—or other seasonal devotions or prayers—to begin and end the sessions.

- You may want to ask a professional counselor, pastor, or therapist in your church to speak and/or be available for questions at the session(s).

- Your church may want to open the group to anyone in the community who is grieving at the holidays, whatever their experience of loss (divorce, estrangement, loss of job, death of a friend, etc.).

- If you choose to use "Grief at the Holidays" as a single session, choose one opening prayer and one closing prayer, and combine the three content reviews as you wish to create a 60- or 90-minute session.

Leader Self-care

(A guide for your spiritual preparation prior to beginning "Grief at the Holidays")

We have different gifts that are consistent with God's grace that has been given to us. . . . If your gift is service, devote yourself to serving. If your gift is teaching, devote yourself to teaching.
Romans 12:6a-7 CEB

Day 1:
Reflect: "God is our refuge and strength, a very present help in trouble" (Psalm 46:1 NRSV).

Read: Introduction to Grief at the Holidays—*Participant Book,* pages 173–75

Pray: Pray that God will be your refuge and help.

Day 2:
Reflect: "Rest in the LORD and wait patiently for him" (Psalm 37:7 KJV).

Read: The Season—*Participant Book,* pages 175–77 (to Personal Reflections)

Pray: Pray for wisdom as you wait on God.

Day 3:
Reflect: "But the path of the righteous is like the light of dawn, which shines brighter and brighter until full day" (Proverbs 4:18 NRSV).

Read: The Season—*Participant Book,* pages 178–79 ("Decide about traditions" to end)

Pray: Pray that through your leadership God will shine the light of dawn on the members of the group.

Day 4:
Reflect: "For you have delivered my soul from death, and my feet from falling, so that I may walk before God in the light of life" (Psalm 56:13 NRSV).

Read: The Experience—*Participant Book,* pages 179–80 (to Personal Reflections)

Pray: Pray that you walk in the light of life.

Day 5:
Reflect: "And let the peace of Christ rule in your hearts.... And be thankful" (Colossians 3:15 NRSV).

Read: The Experience—*Participant Book,* pages 180–82 ("Within the festival" to end)

Pray: Pray that your leadership will herald peace.

Day 6:
Reflect: "Hope in God, for I shall again praise Him, for the help of His presence" (Psalm 42:5 NASB).

Read: The Light—*Participant Book,* pages 182–83

Pray: Pray for the help of God's presence.

Day 7:
Reflect: "May those who sow in tears reap with shouts of joy" (Psalm 126:5 NRSV).

Read: Review The Light—*Participant Book,* pages 182–83

Pray: Pray that God will use your leadership to bring joy.

Session Outline

1. The Season

Greeting (3-4 minutes)

- Begin with a warm word of greeting and inclusion to the entire group. There may be some in attendance who participated in the first eight sessions; or this may be an entirely different group if your church includes anyone in the community who is grieving at the holidays, whatever their experience of loss (divorce, estrangement, loss of job, death of a friend, etc.).

- Remember that, for many, being "welcomed" to a grief group may create resistance, especially at the holiday season. Most participants are struggling with the reality of loneliness and loss at this time of the year.

- Take a few minutes to review and establish the ground rules for the group (see page 36). You may want to distribute copies. Keep extras for those who join the group later if you will be having more than one session of "Grief at the Holidays."

- Participants visibly relax when they know that there is safety in the group and structure for the group.

Opening Prayer (1–2 minutes)
Use or adapt the following prayer, choose a meditation from *Beyond the Broken Heart: Daily Devotions for Your Grief Journey* (see the section Grief Is Celebration, pages 189–207), offer a prayer of your own, or invite a group member to pray.

God, we are here today because we need a special measure of your comfort and peace at the holiday season. We are fearful about what is to come. We do not know how things will be because of our loss. We do know that we are in pain. We listen and hear your assurance, "For I, the Lord your God, hold your right hand; it is I who say to you, 'Do not fear, I will help you'"(Isaiah 41:13 NRSV). We pray for courage to claim your promise. Amen.

Guest Speaker (optional, 8–10 minutes)
Use the time allotted to the video (sessions 1-8) for a guest speaker if you choose to have one. Ask your guest to offer his or her credentials and some personal

comments about the session theme before proceeding to the content review. Determine in advance whether your guest will present the content review or follow your lead, interjecting comments as appropriate.

Content Review
(90-minute session: 30 minutes; 60-minute session: 15–18 minutes)

The Season
- Read aloud the following scripture:

  Be strong and of good courage, do not fear or be in dread ... for it is the LORD your God who goes with you; he will not fail you or forsake you. (Deuteronomy 31:6 RSV)

- Emphasize these points about the holidays:
  - We cannot avoid the holidays; they are part of the rhythm life.
  - Even under the best circumstances, holidays are usually emotion-laden occasions.
  - With the rapid succession of Thanksgiving, Christmas, and the New Year, November and December can be a prolonged period of pain and remembrance.
  - We may dread the unavoidable holiday pressure to do, buy, and experience urged upon us during the season.
  - Our experience of the holidays is intensified because they remind us of our loss.

- Affirm these suggestions about the holidays:
  - If you are uncontrollably tearful or depressed or having suicidal thoughts, this is the time to find a thoughtful, empathetic listener.
  - Being in a support group prior to the holidays is a helpful outlet for expressing your seasonal sadness.
  - It is usually beneficial to cry in the comfort and care of those who understand and may be feeling the same way.
  - It is often the case that when you release your tears, you experience both physical and emotional relief.
    - Remember that your tears may cue family members to express their emotions as well.
    - Some people worry excessively about crying in front of other people.
    - Suppressing your tears at the holidays compounds your pain rather than easing it through the release of heartfelt tears.

- Read aloud the following scripture:

  I commend you because you remember me in everything and maintain the traditions just as I handed them on to you. (1 Corinthians 11:2 NRSV)

- Review these specific coping strategies for the holidays:
  - Put the day in perspective.
    - The actual holiday is just one day.
  - Know your limits.
    - Determine how much or how little you want to do.
  - Plan.
    - Make a plan for the holidays.
  - Take care of yourself.
    - Consider having a "good enough" holiday.
  - Decide about traditions.
    - Create new traditions or modify your old traditions.
  - Be realistic about family.
    - Gatherings may be difficult.

- Affirm these self-care suggestions for the holidays:
  - Get enough rest.
    - The holidays are draining: physically, emotionally, mentally, and spiritually.
    - If you experience any heart-related symptoms, seek immediate medical treatment.
  - Have realistic expectations for yourself and for the day.
  - Be aware that the holidays are the most stressful time of the year.

- Highlight these points about family interactions:
  - Your family may want everything "back to normal."
  - You may experience subtle pressure to be appropriately cheerful.
  - You may be expected to "be over it."
  - Grief may make it difficult for you to participate fully in the festivities.
  - Let others know that they are not responsible for making you happy.
  - You do not have to be happy.
  - Often divorce, blended families, dysfunctional relationships, addictions, and ordinary bad behavior prevent families from sharing a loving, joyful holiday celebration.

- As time allows, use one or more of these questions modified from the Personal Reflections on page 179 of the *Participant Book* (or others of your choosing) to lead a short discussion about the holidays:

❖ What am I dreading about the holiday season?
❖ What is the reality of the "picture" this year?
❖ Why am I afraid of the reality?

Discussion and Sharing
(90-minute session: 30–35 minutes; 60-minute session: 15 minutes)

If you are leading one session on The Season, use this time to engage the group in a discussion about the physical and emotional effects of the holidays using several of these questions modified from the Personal Reflections on page 177 of the *Participant Book* (or others of your choosing):
- Do you have trouble sleeping?
- Do you overeat or have no appetite?
- Do you worry constantly?
- Do you have increased heart rate or rapid breathing while at rest?
- Are you irritable, angry, or impatient?
- Are you tired?
- Are you unable to concentrate?
- Are you guarding your heart?
- Are you taking time for yourself?

Summary Statement and Scripture (2 minutes)
- There is no right or wrong way to experience the holidays, the season, or the actual twenty-four-hour day.
- Acknowledge that the holidays may not be easy for you.
- When you are grieving a loss at the holidays, do the things that are special or important to you.
- Try to do your best for just this one holiday; there will be other holidays.

I will be with you; I will not fail you or forsake you. (Joshua 1:5NRSV)

Closing Prayer (1–3 Minutes)
Use or adapt the following prayer, choose a meditation from *Beyond the Broken Heart: Daily Devotions for Your Grief Journey* (see the section Grief Is Celebration, pages 189–207), offer a prayer of your own, or invite a group member to pray. Or, if your group prefers, allow the group to share prayer concerns and pray for one another.

God, we are grateful for the wisdom and insight offered by a community of support as we share with others who understand our fear and pain. We know that your steadfast love and faithfulness light our way through the darkness of the holiday season. We pray for thoughtful moments to reflect, and quiet within our hearts so that we may listen for your peace. Amen.

Session Outline

2. The Experience

Greeting (3-4 minutes)

- Begin with a warm word of greeting and inclusion to the entire group. There may be some in attendance who participated in the first eight sessions; or this may be an entirely different group if your church includes anyone in the community who is grieving at the holidays, whatever their experience of loss (divorce, estrangement, loss of job, death of a friend, etc.).

- Remember that, for many, being "welcomed" to a grief group may create resistance, especially at the holiday season. Most participants are struggling with the reality of loneliness and loss at this time of the year.

- Take a few minutes to review and establish the ground rules for the group (see page 36). You may want to distribute copies. Keep extras for those who join the group later if you will be having more than one session of "Grief at the Holidays."

- Participants visibly relax when they know that there is safety in the group and structure for the group.

Opening Prayer (1–2 minutes)
Use or adapt the following prayer, choose a meditation from *Beyond the Broken Heart: Daily Devotions for Your Grief Journey* (see the section Grief Is Celebration, pages 189–207), offer a prayer of your own, or invite a group member to pray.

God, as we grieve at Christmas, we remember the past with intense yearning for our loved one, whose presence brought such joy to our life. Even though we sorrow, we seek the experience of Christmas in the gift of your love to us in Christ. We pray that you will surprise us with your comfort as we honor our memories and live today in expectation and hope. Amen.

Guest Speaker (optional, 8–10 minutes)
Use the time allotted to the video (sessions 1-8) for a guest speaker if you choose to have one. Ask your guest to offer his or her credentials and some personal comments about the session theme before proceeding to the content review. Determine in advance whether your guest will present the content review or follow your lead, interjecting comments as appropriate.

Content Review

(90-minute session: 30 minutes; 60-minute session: 15–18 minutes)

The Experience

- Read aloud the following scripture:

  To you is born this day in the city of David a Savior, who is the Messiah, the Lord. (Luke 2:11 NRSV)

- Affirm these points about the two ways in which many people celebrate Christmas:
  - ✤ The festival of Christmas:
    - – The festival celebrates the season and day.
    - – Our secular reference for the festival is tradition.
    - – We struggle with traditions after a loss.
    - – We grieve because we realize that the festival will never be the same again.
  - ✤ The experience of Christmas:
    - – The experience of Christmas may surprise us with the mystery of comfort.
    - – The moment of Christmas may take our breath away with its life-renewing peace.
    - – The experience of Christmas may come to us any day, not just on December 25.
        Expect it.
        Look for it.
        Be open to it.
    - – Christmas comes when someone reaches out to us in love.
    - – Christmas comes when we reach out to someone in love.
    - – Expect an unexpected blessing.
    - – Be a blessing to others.

- Highlight these points about God's love:
  - ✤ When the gift of God's love reaches into our heart, we are certain of life beyond death.
  - ✤ This is the love that holds us close in grief and loss.
  - ✤ This is the love that restores us and makes us whole again.
  - ✤ Christmas means Emmanuel, God with us.
  - ✤ God is with us at Christmas and always,
    - – to comfort us
    - – to redeem us
    - – to restore us

– to give us peace
– to hold us in the communion of saints with the one we have loved and lost

Discussion and Sharing
(90-minute session: 30–35 minutes; 60-minute session: 15 minutes)

If you are leading one session on The Experience, use this time to engage the group in a discussion on the difference between the festival of Christmas and the spiritual experience of Christmas. Guide the exchange of thoughts and ideas so that an equal amount of time is focused on the spiritual experience of Christmas. Use one or more of the following questions modified from the Personal Reflections on page 180 of the *Participant Book* (or others of your choosing) to start the conversation:

- Is it too much effort to put up a tree?
- Will you decorate, or should the ornaments stay packed away this year?
- Is it too painful for you to send Christmas cards?
- Is gift selection a daunting task without the one who is no longer here?

Summary Statement and Scripture (2 minutes)
- Within the festival, our heart seeks the deeper experience of Christmas.
- This yearning is the spiritual need to experience the joy of Christmas.
- Christmas comes in small, private moments when our heart is strangely touched by joy.
- Grief is an opportunity to discover anew the true meaning of Christmas— God's love for humankind.

But the angel said to them, "Do not be afraid; for see—I am bringing you good news of great joy for all the people." (Luke 2:10 NRSV)

Closing Prayer (1–3 Minutes)
Use or adapt the following prayer, choose a meditation from *Beyond the Broken Heart: Daily Devotions for Your Grief Journey* (see the section Grief Is Celebration, pages 189–207), offer a prayer of your own, or invite a group member to pray. Or, if your group prefers, allow the group to share prayer concerns and pray for one another.

God, amid the noise and insistence of the world, especially at the holiday season, we pray that in our grief we may discover anew the true meaning of Christmas. You have given us the greatest gift of all, your love in Christ and the love of the one we will always remember. We pray that you will reach into our hearts with the assurance that you are with us, Emmanuel. Amen.

Session Outline

3. The Light

Greeting (3-4 minutes)

- Begin with a warm word of greeting and inclusion to the entire group. There may be some in attendance who participated in the first eight sessions; or this may be an entirely different group if your church includes anyone in the community who is grieving at the holidays, whatever their experience of loss (divorce, estrangement, loss of job, death of a friend, etc.).

- Remember that, for many, being "welcomed" to a grief group may create resistance, especially at the holiday season. Most participants are struggling with the reality of loneliness and loss at this time of the year.

- Take a few minutes to review and establish the ground rules for the group (see page 36). You may want to distribute copies. Keep extras for those who join the group later if you will be having more than one session of "Grief at the Holidays."

- Participants visibly relax when they know that there is safety in the group and structure for the group.

Opening Prayer (1–2 minutes)
Use or adapt the following prayer, choose a meditation from *Beyond the Broken Heart: Daily Devotions for Your Grief Journey* (see the section Grief Is Celebration, pages 189–207), offer a prayer of your own, or invite a group member to pray.

God, at this holy time, we seek the mystery and miracle of Christmas, your love for us in Christ. We pray that your light will shine into the darkness of our grieving hearts now and in the days ahead. Because you have come to us in Christ, we are certain that death is not the end. We give you thanks for your gifts of love and eternal life in Christ. Amen.

Guest Speaker (optional, 8–10 minutes)
Use the time allotted to the video (sessions 1-8) for a guest speaker if you choose to have one. Ask your guest to offer his or her credentials and some personal comments about the session's theme before proceeding to the content review. Determine in advance whether your guest will present the content review or follow your lead, interjecting comments as appropriate.

Content Review
(90-minute session: 30 minutes; 60-minute session: 15–18 minutes)

The Light
- Read aloud the following scripture:

  The people who walked in darkness have seen a great light; those who dwelt in the land of the shadow of death, upon them a light has shined. (Isaiah 9:2 NKJV)

- Affirm these points about light:
  + Each Christmas light is a brilliant celebration of life.
  + Our reality is that loss and grief have darkened our life.
  + At Christmas, darkness seeks the light and becomes the light.
  + Light shines with the promise that there is life beyond the darkness of loss and grief.
  + Christmas is about the light of the world.
  + The light of God's love illuminates our darkness.
  + Light is the reason for Christmas.

- Emphasize these points about the darkness of chaos:
  + At Christmas, chaos can roil our emotions.
  + There may be chaos in our family or home.
  + The clamor of the secular world may incite chaos in our heart.
  + Light overwhelms and defeats chaos.

- Read aloud this scripture:

  Light dawns for the righteous, and joy for the upright in heart. (Psalm 97:11 NRSV)

- Affirm these emotions of light:
  + Light is in the delicate balance between our sadness and hope for the future.
  + Light is in our heightened peace as we move toward acceptance.
  + Light is in our enjoyment of one or two aspects of the holiday season.
  + Light is in surviving the holidays largely intact.
  + Light is in our understanding of the gift—joy.

- Make the point that darkness is overcome by light:
  + Grief may seem like an eternal night.
  + In loss and grief our light seems overcome for a while by darkness.
  + We have the power to direct our grief as we direct the light.

✤ When we block the light and choose darkness, we become holiday victims.
✤ In darkness there is no light.
✤ Finding the light means managing the darkness.
✤ If we live in darkness, overwhelmed by negative emotions, we should seek help.
✤ We conquer darkness when we allow another to guide us back into the light.
✤ With light, each day holds the promise of remembrance, release, and expression.

Discussion and Sharing
(90-minute session: 30–35 minutes; 60-minute session: 15 minutes)

If you are leading a single session on The Light, use this time to engage the group in a discussion about directing and managing light at the holiday season using one or more of these questions modified from the Personal Reflections on page 183 of the *Participant Book* (or others of your choosing):
• How are you seeking the light at Christmas?
• What manifestations of light minister to you as you grieve at Christmas?
• Do you dwell in darkness, resisting the light?
• How do you direct the light to shine into your grief?

Summary Statement and Scripture (2 minutes)
• We receive the blessing of Christmas when moments of light shine in our heart.
    ✤ Light shines in quiet meditation.
    ✤ Light shines in moments of prayer and thanksgiving.
• We are at peace in the certainty that loss and death are not the end.
• We know that our shared light shines forever.
• We celebrate new life in the light of God's love in Christ.
• We walk in the light.

For you have delivered my soul from death, and my feet from falling, so that I may walk before God in the light of life. (Psalm 56:13 NRSV)

Closing Prayer (1–3 Minutes)
Use or adapt the following prayer, choose a meditation from *Beyond the Broken Heart: Daily Devotions for Your Grief Journey* (see the section Grief Is Celebration, pages 189–207), offer a prayer of your own, or invite a group member to pray. Or, if your group prefers, allow the group to share prayer concerns and pray for one another.

God, at Christmas we pray that the light of your love for us will reach into every corner of our heart to illuminate the darkness of our grief. We know that because you are with us in Christ, you hold us close in our sadness and sorrow at this season and always. We pray that in Emmanuel we may understand that in you we find everlasting love and joy. Amen.

SESSION 10 – PEACE OF MIND: FINANCIAL MANAGEMENT FOR LIFE

(1 or More Sessions)

How to Use This Material

- You may want to ask a tax advisor (CPA), certified financial planner, attorney, or estate planning specialist in your church or community to partner with you to lead the group. As a complement to your spiritual guidance of the group, a professional could present the content and/or be available for questions during the session.

- If you decide to ask a professional who works in the financial services industry to lead the content review for the session, it is important that he or she understands that the group is not an opportunity to promote or sell products or services.

- For this session your church might want to open the group to anyone in the community who is struggling with financial management because of a death or loss (death of a loved one, divorce, separation, loss of job, etc.).

- The session content review can be completed in one 90-minute session, or it can be divided into two or more sessions with "homework" assignments for participants to complete between sessions using the forms and worksheets provided in the Appendix.

- If you plan to have more than one session, use the short meditations in *Beyond the Broken Heart: Daily Devotions for Your Grief Journey* (see the section Grief Is Hope pages 109–24)—or other devotions or prayers on stewardship—to begin and end the sessions.

Leader Self-care

(A guide for your spiritual preparation prior to beginning "Peace of Mind")

If your gift is encouragement, devote yourself to encouraging. The one giving should do it with no strings attached. The leader should lead with passion. The one showing mercy should be cheerful.
Romans 12:8 CEB

Day 1:
Reflect: "I have been young, and now am old, yet I have not seen the righteous forsaken or their children begging bread. They are ever giving liberally and lending, and their children become a blessing" (Psalm 37:25-26 NRSV).

Read: Introduction to Peace of Mind—*Participant Book,* pages 187–89

Pray: Pray that your leadership is strong in assurance.

Day 2:
Reflect: "For by the grace given to me I say to everyone among you not to think of yourself more highly than you ought to think, but to think with sober judgment, each according to the measure of faith that God has assigned" (Romans 12:3 NRSV).

Read: Personal Business Management—*Participant Book,* pages 189–92 (through Step 1: Assessment)

Pray: Pray for humility; lead through your faith.

Day 3:
Reflect: "Moreover, it is required of stewards that they be found trustworthy" (1 Corinthians 4:2 NRSV).

Read: Personal Business Management—*Participant Book,* page 192 (Step 2: Organization)

Pray: Pray that your leadership is trustworthy.

Day 4:
Reflect: "Teach me knowledge and good judgment, for I trust your commands" (Psalm 119:66 NIV).

Read: Personal Business Management—*Participant Book,* pages 192–93 (Step 3: Inventory)

Pray: Pray that God will bless you with knowledge and good judgment.

Day 5:
Reflect: "In quietness and confidence shall be your strength" (Isaiah 30:15 NKJV).

Read: Personal Business Management—*Participant Book,* page 193 (Step 4: Analysis)

Pray: Pray for a quiet, confident spirit.

Day 6:
Reflect: "And you will have confidence, because there is hope; you will be protected and take your rest in safety" (Job 11:18 NRSV).

Read: Review Forms and Worksheets—*Participant Book,* pages 194–98

Pray: Pray that God will fill you with hope.

Day 7:
Reflect: "My goal is that their hearts would be encouraged and united together in love, so that they might have all the riches of assurance that come with understanding, so that they might have the knowledge of the secret plan of God, namely Christ" (Colossians 2:2 CEB).

Read: Action Plan—*Participant Book,* pages 199–201

Pray: Pray that your leadership will encourage and unite the group in love.

Session Outline

Greeting (3-4 minutes)

- Begin with a warm word of greeting and inclusion to the entire group. There may be some in attendance who participated in the other sessions of the program; or this may be an entirely different group if your church includes anyone in the community interested in financial management because of a death or loss (death of a loved one, divorce, separation, loss of job, etc.).

- Remember that, for many, being "welcomed" to a group may create resistance. Be sensitive to the anxiety level of the group. Some participants may feel overwhelmed by their financial condition; you may sense an undercurrent of quiet desperation. Use confident words to express hope and reassurance; acknowledge that there may be some in the group struggling with grief, loneliness, and loss.

- Take a few minutes to review and establish the ground rules for the group (see page 36). You may want to distribute copies. Keep extras for those who join the group later if you will be having more than one session of "Peace of Mind."

- Participants visibly relax when they know that there is safety in the group and structure for the group.

Opening Prayer (1–2 minutes)
Use the following prayer or adapt the words and spiritual direction to your personal prayer vocabulary.

God, we are here today because we need help with the financial management of our lives. We bring our fears, our anxieties, and our desperation to you; we pray that you will open our eyes to what we must do to help ourselves. We believe that you will strengthen us and help us through the power and presence of the Holy Spirit with us. Amen.

Guest Speaker (optional, 8–10 minutes)
Use the time allotted for the video (sessions 1-8) for a guest speaker if you choose to have one. Ask your guest to offer his or her credentials and some personal comments about the session theme before proceeding to the content review. Determine in advance whether your guest will present the content review or follow your lead, interjecting comments as appropriate.

Content Review
(90-minute session: 30 minutes; 60-minute session: 15–18 minutes)

- Read aloud the following scripture:

  For God has not given us a spirit of fear, but of power and of love and of a sound mind. (2 Timothy 1:7 NKJV)

- Affirm these points:
  - ✤ Financial management can be a daunting challenge for anyone at any time of life.
    - – It is especially important with advancing age, in the event of illness, at the death of a loved one, or when some other life-altering loss or change occurs.
    - – Personal business and financial management may seem overwhelming at a time of grief or life loss.
  - ✤ You may lack information and understanding, which may cause you to feel anxious and helpless.
    - – *Not knowing* causes fear, which is part of every crisis in life.
  - ✤ The information in this session is very basic.
    - – It is not about creating or amassing wealth.
    - – It is about empowering you to manage successfully what you have.
  - ✤ There is no performance standard for the task of financial management.
    - – You start where you are.
    - – You start with what you have.
    - – You learn.
    - – If you are willing, you can do it.

- Highlight these desired outcomes:
  - ✤ Relief from chaos
    - – Simplified financial understanding and management provides relief from chaos.
  - ✤ Reassurance
    - – You *can* manage and master your finances.
  - ✤ Peace
    - – Peace of mind gives continuity to your life.

- Emphasize this important point:
  - ✤ *No one cares about your money as much as you care about your money.*

- Affirm that several factors influence your emotions about finances and money:

- ✦ Money attitudes learned from others:
  - how your parents communicated about money
  - how you communicate/communicated with your spouse about money
  - your own self-confidence in personal money management
- ✦ Your actual financial condition:
  - your realistic understanding of your assets and liabilities
  - your commitment to living within your means

- Emphasize that managing money positively and proactively has these benefits:
  - ✦ Empowerment—having control over that which is quantifiable (money)
  - ✦ Peace of mind—learning hands-on management (finance and business)
    - you understand what resources are available for your use (income)
    - you take charge of your day-to-day personal business administration (budgeting)
  - ✦ Financial independence

- Review these four essential steps to simplifying financial management:
  - ✦ Assessment
    - Tackle the everyday tasks—pay the bills on time.
    - Simplify your business management.
  - ✦ Organization
    - Get your information together.
    - Have a filing system that works for you.
  - ✦ Inventory
    - Make a list of your assets and liabilities—what you have and what you owe.
  - ✦ Analysis
    - Look at your assets and liabilities—understand what your standard of living should be.
    - Make a budget.
    - Live within your means.

- Review these points about ongoing business management:
  - ✦ Review and update your information at least once a year.
  - ✦ Work with professional advisors, your children, or trusted friends to evaluate your finances and make strategic recommendations if necessary.

    ✦ Incorporate business management into your life without allowing it to take on more significance than it should.
    ✦ The goal is peace of mind.

- As time allows, use one or more of the following suggestions (from the Action Plan on pages 199–201 of the *Participant Book*) to lead a short discussion about practical safety:
  ✦ Do you have a home fire extinguisher?
  ✦ Does your house have a smoke detector/alarm?
  ✦ If you live alone, should you consider having a personal in-home monitoring system?
  ✦ Do you have a 24-hour pharmacy?
  ✦ Do you have a medical condition for which you should wear a medic alert bracelet?

Discussion and Sharing
(90-minute session: 30–35 minutes; 60-minute session: 15 minutes)

Use this time to talk with the group about the completion of the forms and worksheets (see pages 136–40 in this book, and pages 194–98 in the *Participant Book*). If there will be more than one session of "Peace of Mind," participants may finish the worksheets after class as their "homework." For now, they are to begin working on the Personal Monthly Management Budget.

- Distribute pencils and copies of the Personal Monthly Management Budget (pages 139–40).

- Explain what each line means and ask participants to enter an exact or estimated amount.
  ✦ Participants may know some of this information without needing to refer to their records.

- Remind participants that this information is confidential and only for their own information.
  ✦ Affirm that they will not be asked to share any personal details with the group.

Summary Statement and Scripture (2 minutes)
- Money management is business.
- Business does not merit an investment of your emotional energy.

- You prepare a comprehensive, permanent record of personal and business information:
  - ✦ for your own reference
  - ✦ for those who assist you
  - ✦ for those who will settle your estate
- Your business is the material estate you endow as part of your lasting legacy.
- Financial management honors the trust of your loved one and builds for the future.
- Your stewardship of earthly resources blesses those you love for generations to come.
- Financial management enables you to meet both opportunity and adversity with peace of mind.

In peace I will both lie down and sleep; for thou alone, O LORD, makest me dwell in safety. (Psalm 4:8 RSV)

Closing Prayer (1–3 Minutes)
Use the following prayer, offer one of your own, or invite a group member to pray. Or, if your group prefers, allow the group to share prayer concerns and pray for one another.

God, we depart today with greater peace of mind because we know that you are with us as we struggle and strive to make sense of the business of this world. We pray that you will give comfort and courage to those among us who are grieving. We pray that you will give strength and wisdom to those among us who are adjusting to a new way of life because of losses other than death. Bless us as we seek a life of stewardship and peace. Amen.

APPENDIX

Promotional Copy for
Newsletter or Website

How do you understand grief when your heart is broken by the death of a loved one? To survive and live forward, those who grieve must find answers. Beyond the Broken Heart is a support group for those who are grieving the death of a loved one and are in need of a community to share the loneliness of grief. Scriptural wisdom will be used to explore the issues of grief and offer spiritual encouragement for a life of renewed hope and joy. The group will also offer some specific coping strategies to guide the way back to fullness of life. If you are grieving the death of a loved one, please join us on the journey through grief.

Meeting Dates:

Time:

Location:

For more information, contact:

Bulletin Announcement

How do you understand grief when your heart is broken by the death of a loved one? If you are grieving the death of a loved one, please join us on the journey through grief in a Beyond the Broken Heart support group to share the loneliness of your grief. Scriptural wisdom will be used to explore the spiritual issues of grief and offer encouragement for a life of renewed hope and joy. The group will also offer some specific coping strategies to guide the way back to fullness of life. The group will meet on (*day and/or dates*) from (*start time*) to (*end time*). To register, please contact (*group leader or contact person*) at (*phone number*), or simply come and be part of our grief community.

Overview of Assets, Liabilities, Income

ASSETS

1. BANK ACCOUNTS
NAME OF ACCOUNT HOLDER(S)_____
NAME OF INSTITUTION_____
ACCOUNT NUMBER/STYLE   SIGNATORIES
CHECKING_____
     APPROXIMATE BALANCE_____
MONEY MARKET SAVINGS_____
     APPROXIMATE BALANCE_____
CERTIFICATE OF DEPOSIT_____
     FACE VALUE_____
     INTEREST RATE_____
     MATURITY DATE_____
     INTEREST_____

2. BROKERAGE ACCOUNTS_____
NAME OF ACCOUNT HOLDER_____
NAME OF INSTITUTION_____
SECURITIES HELD   SHARES   APPROXIMATE VALUE
STOCKS_____
     _____
BONDS_____
     _____
MUTUAL FUNDS_____
     _____
MONEY MARKET ACCOUNT(S)_____
     _____

3. MUTUAL FUND/INDIVIDUAL STOCK ACCOUNTS
NAME OF FUND/STOCK_____
     NUMBER OF SHARES HELD/FUND BALANCE_____
     NAME OF ACCOUNT HOLDER_____
     PARTICIPANT NUMBER_____
     NAME OF INSTITUTION_____

Reproduced by permission from Julie Yarbrough, *Beyond the Broken Heart: A Journey Through Grief, Leader Guide* (Nashville: Abingdon Press, 2012).

LIABLITIES

MORTGAGE LOANS:

    HOMESTEAD_____ $_____

    SECOND HOME_____ $_____

    RENTAL PROPERTIES_____ $_____

    HOME EQUITY LOAN_____ $_____

AUTOMOBILE LOANS/LEASES_____ $_____

CREDIT CARD DEBT_____ $_____

NOTES PAYABLE_____ $_____

LOANS FROM BROKERAGE MARGIN ACCOUNT_____ $_____

BANK LOANS_____ $_____

UNPAID/DEFERRED IRS TAX LIABILITY_____ $_____

ESTIMATE OF TOTAL LIABILITIES _____ $_____

NET WORTH = ASSETS MINUS LIABILITIES_____ $_____

ESTIMATE OF NET WORTH_____ $_____

INCOME

SALARY AND BONUSES_____ $_____

DEFERRED COMPENSATION_____ $_____

SOCIAL SECURITY_____ $_____

PENSION PLAN_____ $_____

INVESTMENT INCOME_____ $_____

IRA_____ $_____

ALIMONY_____ $_____

CHILD SUPPORT_____ $_____

ESTIMATE OF TOTAL INCOME PER YEAR_____ $_____

ESTIMATE OF INCOME TAXES OWED PER YEAR_____ $_____

ESTIMATE OF NET INCOME PER YEAR _____ $_____

ESTIMATE OF TOTAL INCOME PER MONTH_____ $_____

Reproduced by permission from Julie Yarbrough, *Beyond the Broken Heart: A Journey Through Grief, Leader Guide* (Nashville: Abingdon Press, 2012).

Personal Financial Inventory

ASSETS

CHECKING ACCOUNT(S)_____ $_____
SAVINGS ACCOUNT(S)_____ $_____
CERTIFICATES OF DEPOSIT_____ $_____
MONEY MARKET FUNDS_____ $_____
INVESTMENTS:
    STOCKS_____ $_____
    BONDS_____ $_____
    MUTUAL FUNDS_____ $_____
    IRA_____ $_____
ANNUITIES_____ $_____
LIFE INSURANCE AND DEATH BENEFITS_____ $_____
COMPANY BENEFITS:
    STOCK OPTIONS_____ $_____
    SAVINGS/401(k) PLANS_____ $_____
    ESOP/PAYSOP_____ $_____
    PENSION PLAN_____ $_____
    DEFERRED COMPENSATION_____ $_____
REAL ESTATE:
    HOMESTEAD_____ $_____
    SECOND HOME_____ $_____
    RENTAL PROPERTIES_____ $_____
    MORTGAGES/DEEDS RECEIVABLE_____ $_____
REAL PROPERTY:
    OIL AND GAS INTERESTS_____ $_____
    PARTNERSHIP INTERESTS_____ $_____
PERSONAL PROPERTY:
    FINE ART_____ $_____
    JEWELRY_____ $_____
    HOUSEHOLD FURNISHINGS _____ $_____
    AUTOMOBILES_____ $_____
    OTHER PERSONAL EFFECTS_____ $_____
ESTIMATE OF TOTAL ASSETS_____ **$_____**

Reproduced by permission from Julie Yarbrough, *Beyond the Broken Heart: A Journey Through Grief, Leader Guide* (Nashville: Abingdon Press, 2012).

Personal Monthly Management Budget

GROSS INCOME

SALARY/WAGES/COMPENSATION_____ $_____
SOCIAL SECURITY_____ $_____
IRA_____ $_____
ANNUITY_____ $_____
PENSION PLAN_____ $_____
INVESTMENT INCOME_____ $_____
ESTIMATE OF TOTAL GROSS MONTHLY INCOME____ $_____
ESTIMATE OF TOTAL GROSS ANNUAL INCOME _____$_____

EXPENSES

HOUSING:
    RENT/MORTGAGE_____ $_____
    ASSOCIATION FEES OR DUES_____ $_____
    INSURANCE_____ $_____
    TAXES _____ $_____
    HOME MAINTENANCE_____ $_____
    UTILITIES:
        GAS_____ $_____
        ELECTRICITY_____ $_____
        WATER_____ $_____
        TELEPHONE_____ $_____
        CABLE/INTERNET SERVICE_____ $_____
CREDIT CARD/INSTALLMENT DEBT_____ $_____
STUDENT/EDUCATION LOANS_____ $_____
TRANSPORTATION:
    AUTOMOBILE LOAN/LEASE PAYMENT_____ $_____
    GAS/MAINTENANCE_____ $_____
    INSURANCE_____ $_____
FOOD_____ $_____
MEDICAL_____ $_____
WORK-RELATED EXPENSES _____ $_____

Reproduced by permission from Julie Yarbrough, *Beyond the Broken Heart: A Journey Through Grief, Leader Guide* (Nashville: Abingdon Press, 2012).

PENSION/401(k) CONTRIBUTION_____ $_____
IRA CONTRIBUTION_____ $_____
SAVINGS_____ $_____
SUPPORT OF DEPENDENT(S)_____ $_____
TAXES:
     PROPERTY TAXES_____ $_____
     INCOME TAXES_____ $_____
CHARITABLE CONTRIBUTIONS_____ $_____
INSURANCE:
     LIFE INSURANCE_____ $_____
     HEALTH INSURANCE_____ $_____
     LONG-TERM CARE INSURANCE_____ $_____
     UMBRELLA LIABILITY INSURANCE_____ $_____
     PROPERTY INSURANCE:_____ $_____
        SCHEDULED PROPERTY_____ $_____
        JEWELRY_____ $_____
PERSONAL EXPENSES:
     CLOTHING_____ $_____
     ENTERTAINMENT_____ $_____
     TRAVEL_____ $_____
     EDUCATION_____ $_____
     GIFTS_____ $_____
     PERSONAL ITEMS_____ $_____
ESTIMATE OF TOTAL MONTHLY EXPENSES_____$_____
ESTIMATE OF TOTAL ANNUAL EXPENSES_____$_____

Reproduced by permission from Julie Yarbrough, *Beyond the Broken Heart:
A Journey Through Grief, Leader Guide* (Nashville: Abingdon Press, 2012).

Notes

1. James Dalton Morrison, ed., *Masterpieces of Religious Verse* (New York: Harper Brothers Publishers, 1948), 342.

2. *The American Heritage Dictionary of the English Language, Fourth Edition,* (Boston: Houghton Mifflin harcourt, 2006), s.v. "fear."

3. Jan Richardson, *In Wisdom's Path* (Cleveland: Pilgrim Press, 2000), 124.

4. *Roget's II: The New Thesaurus, Third Edition* (Boston: Houston Mifflin Harcourt, 2003), s.v. "victim."